TELEPLAY

An Introduction to Television Writing

TELEPLAY

An Introduction to Television Writing

Revised Edition

by COLES TRAPNELL

HAWTHORN BOOKS, Inc.
Publishers / New York

TELEPLAY: AN INTRODUCTION TO TELEVISION WRITING

 All inquiries should be addressed to Hawthorn Books, Inc., 260 Madison Avenue, New York, New York 10016. This book was manufactured in the United States of America and published simultaneously in Canada by Prentice-Hall of Canada, Limited, 1870 Birchmount Road, Scarborough, Ontario.

Library of Congress Catalog Card Number: 66–12571
ISBN: O–8015–7486–2
5 6 7 8 9 10

Contents

Preface

If you want to earn a living writing for television, you must have the ability to work very hard for very long periods under very high pressure. You will also need some talent and a knowledge of the teleplay pattern. This book professes to provide certain elements of that knowledge.

For some time I have conducted a television workshop class directed at a group that is rapidly and steadily growing in the land: new young writers who are attracted to the drama as a means of expression and communication rather than to the mediums of the short story and the novel. In this area, television, with its insistent demand for story material in vast quantities, represents the most immediate opportunity for the new writer. Itself a goal for many writers, it can also be a stepping stone for others towards the related levels of stage play and theatrical motion picture.

Our class starts with an examination of basic theater principles, and we finish with our equivalent of a college term paper: an hour-long teleplay with commercial possibilities. We journey to our destination along a road paved with constant writing, some lecturing, readings of work in progress, and uninhibited criticism and analysis of that work.

The book follows the workshop course (including in the second half an inevitable consideration of television marketing opportunities). The fundamentals of television writing are the same as those of any theatrical medium. In this book you will find yourself involved with the stage and with movies as well as with television.

The early chapters explore dramatic principles, and the illustrations are drawn largely from the contemporary theater. I have chosen to refer to several well-known stage plays, rather than to current television scripts, because the plays are superior in quality and fully as pertinent. Also, the dramas discussed will not become out of date in a year or two as would selections from today's television fare. And the plays are readily available for study, either in paperback editions or at the libraries.

As far as the television medium goes, this is a book for beginners. It takes for granted nothing that relates to the construction of a teleplay, a screenplay for television. The reader I intend it for is, like my students, a man or woman who is impelled to write and who wants to master this newest of creative forms. His background may or may not include some writing of fiction and nonfiction prose. He may or may not be familiar with creative writing courses at the college level. Whatever his experience, he is now about to be challenged by a new and exciting and rewarding method of communicating his ideas.

I ask this writer to keep in mind, from the very first page, the literal definition of the Greek word, *drama:* "a deed, an action." Hence, something to be done, something to be performed.

Not just "something to be read."

TELEPLAY

An Introduction to Television Writing

PART ONE

CHIEFLY THEORY

I

Fade In

The Writers Guild favors the word "teleplay" to designate a television script. This differentiates it from "screenplay" which is commonly understood to mean the script for a movie intended to be shown in theaters. The point for us to remember is that "play" is the important part of each word.

If you write for television, you are writing for the theater—or one section of it. You are telling a story in dramatized form. So did Aristophanes and Plautus in the Greek and Roman amphitheaters. So did the miracle playwrights in the market places of the Middle Ages, Shakespeare on his bare platform at the Globe, Sheridan on curtained stages with scenery, all the way down to the twentieth century storytellers who command the scientific resources of stage and screen. Your medium is different. Your story (it is to be hoped) will be seen on an illuminated tube in millions of living rooms instead of on Broadway or off Broadway or on a monsterscope screen in a big movie theater. But you are all doing the same essential thing: *telling a story in dramatic terms.*

So, obviously, there are elements that go into a good play that must also go into a good movie or television script. What will hold an audience in the theater, the climactic scene between the two brothers in O'Neill's *Long Day's Journey into Night,* for instance, will hold them in front of their television screens. As writers, you know that a certain kind of story may be most acceptable for publication, but if it's not right for the stage or for a movie, it is not likely to be right for television. This is a simple and obvious principle. Also basic. And thus worth repeating and pondering.

Later on, we will go into those elements that make a story right for the dramatic forms. For the present, keep in mind that your television story reaches your audience only through what they see your characters do and what they hear them say.

Teleplay Grammar

Your script directions, no matter how vividly presented in eloquent writing, are never going to be read by your audience. You are denied the novelist's tool of descriptive prose. This is no reason to neglect the directions in your script. They can be of great help in showing the producer and director of the finished film exactly *how* you want your story set forth. Conversely, skimping or omitting them at crucial points can result in some pretty peculiar interpretations of what you had in mind. You will find that enough startling changes due to production demands and problems you never dreamed of have occurred between typewriter and picture tube, without your compounding the differences by a paucity of directions. I repeat. To tell your story clearly, interestingly, effectively, you must rely on what your characters are seen to do and what they are heard to say.

While a stage manuscript has much in common with one for a movie or teleplay, there are marked physical differences. I am talking now about the form or pattern of the teleplay—the way the page of a teleplay looks. You use terms like "long shot" and "close-up" to indicate the kind of scene you visualize. You will "dissolve" from one scene to another or "fade out" and "fade in" to show a time lapse. In appearance the teleplay script and the one for the feature screenplay are identical. The screenplay is longer than the hour television script and even longer than the ninety-minute teleplay. This is the only physical difference between the two. The teleplay has inherited the conventions, the grammar, of the older theatrical medium. (So many television shows are filmed or taped now, as compared to the thriving days when *Playhouse 90* and *Studio One* were broadcast live, that it seemed sensible for this book to deal with film. Television shot live is based on a script somewhat different in appearance from the teleplay for film.)

There are two fairly common student attitudes towards the technical demands of writing the teleplay. One is represented by the too-confident writer who thinks that once he has mastered film terms and has learned how to set them down on the page where they belong he knows television writing and is all set. The other extreme is the apprentice with too little confidence. He is terrified by the unfamiliar pattern, and worries about the difference between Reverse Angles and Point of View shots.

Both attitudes are equally wrong.

Of course there is more to television writing than knowing when to go from a long shot to a medium close shot, or when to have the camera move to accompany a walking character. But there is nothing cabalistic or exceedingly difficult about the correct writing down of camera directions, or learning where on the page to set your dialogue and where your directions. Learning the form calls for study, for memorizing, and, above all, for a great deal of practice in putting its elements down on paper. It is like studying Latin grammar, memorizing Latin vocabulary, and practicing translation of Latin sentences before you tackle Caesar's *Gallic War*. Ideally, you should drive and drill yourself until you are so familiar with these terms and how to use them that you can forget them: they should be all but automatic in your writing. It may solace you to hear that a good professional script uses camera terminology most sparingly. It makes no attempt to approximate the huge number of shots the director employs in shooting the picture. A sixty-page teleplay may have as few as seventy-five shots or camera directions in all. We shall consider the reasons for such economy in Chapter VI.

Knowing the Tools

Right now, let's examine some of these not-so-formidable script directions and look at examples of them. The examples will give you a notion of how the material looks on the page, the *typographical* appearance of directions and dialogue.

FADE IN introduces every professional screenplay or teleplay script ever written. It is always written in capital letters, and it appears either at the right or left side of the page. It means simply going from nothing to something, from a blank, dark screen to a picture. The scene doesn't spring out at you instantly. It "fades in" from darkness to light, but the process lasts only one or two seconds. The opening scene of your script should look like this (our examples contain unfamiliar terms, but we'll label them and discuss them as we go along):

FADE IN:

EXT. MERIDIAN STREET   LONG SHOT   DAY

Meridian is a small town in the Iowa of the 1890's. It is shortly after dawn, and few people are on the store-lined street. The stillness is broken by the SOUND of the clop-clop of horses' hooves, and a wagon loaded with hay and pulled by two stout farm horses appears from a side street and heads towards CAMERA. As it approaches, we can see the figure of a young girl seated beside the driver, who is a young man dressed like a farmer.

That first line in capital letters directly following FADE IN is typical in appearance of all headings for camera shots or directions throughout your script. EXT. is the customary abbreviation for EXTERIOR, and you use it to introduce any scene that takes place in a street or a field, on a rooftop, or in any place that is out-of-doors. Its opposite, of course, is INT. (for INTERIOR) and you will use this in the same manner for beginning a sequence that is located in a drawing room, office, auditorium, or the like.

LONG SHOT means what it says: a shot with the camera far enough back from the immediate setting so that the spectator gets an over-all view. It establishes where we are; in the example I gave you we see a large part of a town street.

At the beginning of a sequence (and only at the beginning) you indicate in this capitalized shot-heading whether it is day or night. This direction always comes after the indication of the setting and the shot and is written at the right-hand margin. You don't say "late afternoon" or "dusk" or "later that same day." Just "day" or "night." Studio production departments have to plan a picture in infinite detail to determine how much it will cost. They have made this rule because, among their thousand and one other tasks, they have to enumerate the day sequences and the night ones in all scripts. So when you want to indicate a specific time of day or night, do it in the directions in upper and lower case type that come below the heading. You will notice that I have done this above; the second sentence of the direction says, "It is shortly after dawn . . ."

There is a certain amount of latitude in the terms of the direction headings, and this may make the subject seem a little less forbidding.

Take the scene heading above. Instead of LONG SHOT you might write FULL SHOT or ESTABLISHING SHOT and still be perfectly correct. (ESTABLISHING, however, is generally used only for the opening scene of your teleplay.) And nobody will fault you if you reverse your heading so it reads:

```
LONG SHOT    EXT. MERIDIAN STREET    DAY
```

But there are certain typographical constants observed by all professional teleplay writers, and it is important that you know and practice them. Observing them will make your script look like a professional job when it is submitted to a story editor or producer. Not bothering, getting things wrong here and there, stamps *amateur* on it, a needlessly unfair introduction if the actual content of your teleplay is good.

With the Meridian Street direction as a model, let's take heed of the following:

Leave a space between FADE IN (always capitalized) and the heading (LONG SHOT and the like) of your directions.

The shot heading is written in capital letters. If the heading is too long for one line, put the finish on the next line *without* a space. The second line, not indented, begins directly under the first.

Always leave one space between the heading and the direction itself.

The direction, like its heading, runs the full width of the page between the margins. It is written in capitals and small letters (upper and lower case). It is single-spaced. If the direction is unusually long (as in a scene which has a lot of action unbroken by any dialogue) you can separate it into several parts, with one space between each single-spaced segment. Neither heading nor direction is ever indented like a paragraph; both begin at the inner edge of the left-hand margin.

If you refer to anything audible in your direction, use the word SOUND and capitalize it. (The SOUND of somebody running, the SOUND of distant shouting, or the SOUND of a sudden blast of band music.)

Finally (for this particular example) always capitalize the word CAMERA when you use it.

In connection with this last rule, remember that all directions and descriptions are written *from the camera's viewpoint.* This may seem too obvious to mention, but writers have been known to get mixed up in their geography when describing complicated action. Keep in mind that your directions apply to what the camera sees. This will be what your audience sees when the camera has recorded the action which you have outlined in the directions. Your audience, looking at your picture, *is* the camera. And when we read in the script that "a wagon appears and heads towards CAMERA," it is the same as reading that it heads towards us, the audience.

Just as you always write FADE IN to start your script, you end it with a FADE OUT. Here is what the end of your final script scene should look like:

```
Arnold turns away from the police officer and looks at
Grace, who starts to laugh at his predicament.

                         ARNOLD
                Goodbye, my dear. And watch
                your step. You can see--
                    (glancing wryly
                     at the officer)
                --crime doesn't pay.

                         GRACE
                When will we have you back with
                us?

                         OFFICER
                    (taking Arnold's
                     arm)
                In about sixty days.

Arnold shrugs in dismay, then grins, and allows himself to
be led away by the police officer as we--

                                              FADE OUT


                         THE END
```

The fade in and fade out devices may also be used—sparingly—in the body of your script. They always mean a major transition in the continuity of your story. If you want to indicate a considerable lapse of time, or if you are going to introduce new characters and a new theme, use FADE OUT at the end of the old scene, and FADE IN at the beginning of the new one. Succinctly, the terms are correctly used for a big break in the story line. If your story falls into a three-act or four-act pattern, the fade terms can be used to indicate these act divisions.

Where the Speeches Go

The example I gave above shows the typographical relation between your dialogue and your directions. The dialogue is always narrowly columned in the center of the page (and, like the directions, always single-spaced); the directions always run out farther on each side. The skipping of one space between speeches, and between a direction and a speech, is standard.

A speech is always headed by the name in capitals of the character who delivers it. The only variation to this rule occurs when a speech is given by somebody who is not within camera range. The speaker is O.S. (abbreviation for OFF SCENE). You indicate that he is not in sight when his voice is heard by heading his speech ARNOLD'S VOICE or OFFICER'S VOICE or the voice of whoever is heard but not, at that instant, seen. For example, in the little scene above, Grace might have been outside the range of the camera which was closely concentrating on Arnold and the arresting officer. If so, then you would write her line:

```
             GRACE'S VOICE
When will we have you back with
us?
```

Now you will notice in this same sample scene two or three small directions which are in parentheses and are included in the dialogue. These are standard, too, but you must know when to use them and when not to. They are always phrases or broken sentences, and they are always short—no more than three of those very narrow lines at the most. Occurring at the beginning or in the middle of a character's speech, as they do, they almost always refer to that character. "Glancing wryly at the officer" and "taking Arnold's arm" are typical parenthetical directions.

But suppose you have a much longer direction that you want to insert *while* a character is talking. Then you interrupt him, skip a space for a regular direction (a full sentence, not a phrase), skip another space, and resume his dialogue with a notation that the speech is being continued. Here is how it's done:

```
                                                  DISSOLVE:


INT. THORPE'S LIBRARY    MED. CLOSE SHOT    THORPE    NIGHT

This is a small room with a casement window and most of the
wall space occupied by book shelves. THORPE, a man of fifty,
silver-haired and aristocratic in appearance, is sitting
under a lamp, examining a manuscript. CAMERA ANGLE WIDENS as
the door opens and Sylvia walks in. Thorpe looks up and
smiles with pleasure. He gets to his feet.

                         THORPE
                I thought you were never going
                to show up. Wait till you see
                what I've found.

Walking with a pronounced limp, he crosses to one of the
shelves and takes down a book. Sylvia watches him with a
quizzical look.

                         THORPE
                      (continues)
                When you read this--
                      (leafing through
                       book)
                --you will realize how utterly
                and stupidly wrong you were.
```

So much for the interrupted speech. I have included other elements in this scene fragment with which you had better become familiar before we go any farther.

Camera Terminology

First the DISSOLVE (sometimes written DISSOLVE TO:). You make use of this when you have a story transition (lapse of time or change in locale) less radical than one calling for a fade out and a fade in. In a dissolve, the scene coming up is superimposed on the scene just finishing, and in a second or two the old scene vanishes and the new one becomes sharp and clear. We may imagine that the scene just before the one above ended with Sylvia saying to someone, "Well, I'm off to give old Thorpe a piece of my mind," and as she starts out we DISSOLVE to Thorpe's library a moment before Sylvia comes in.

You will notice that the first time Thorpe is mentioned in the directions, his name appears in capitals. This is because he is a new character whom we haven't seen before. Every time you introduce a character in a script, capitalize all the letters of his name. But only when he is introduced. Thereafter, he is referred to throughout the script, in the directions, in conventional capitals and lower case letters. This applies only to the directions, of course, not to the dialogue pattern: we have already noted that when you give your character something to say, his name should appear all in capitals at the top of his speech. Always give a description—brief, unless a story exigency demands details—when you bring in a character for the first time. Thorpe is "a man of fifty, silver-haired and aristocratic in appearance." Sylvia, obviously, has made her appearance earlier, and we may assume that she has been duly capitalized and described.

Now, according to the direction heading, when we see Thorpe sitting in his library, the camera has photographed him in a medium (MED.) close shot.

This seems like a good place to go over the different shots you will want to use in your scripts. We already know what a long shot is from that 1890 street in Iowa. It shows the audience as much as possible. You would most often use a long shot for an exterior since there is scarcely room in most interiors for a genuine long shot. If it were important to show what kind of house Thorpe lived in, you would precede that library scene with an establishing long shot:

```
EXT. THORPE'S HOUSE    LONG SHOT    NIGHT

This is a mansion at least seventy-five years old, and large
enough to accommodate a small boarding school. The architec-
ture is gingerbread-Gothic. One light is visible, shining out
from a room on the first floor.
```

Next, in terms of diminishing distance, comes the MED. LONG SHOT, with the camera a bit nearer its subject. A MED. LONG SHOT of Thorpe in our sample scene would show us most of the library, the window, door, and bookshelves, with Thorpe in the background.

A MEDIUM SHOT is closer, but still not very close. In it we would see the full-length figure of Thorpe and less of his surroundings. Midway between the long shots and the closer ones, MED. SHOT is a very handy camera position. It could be used to show a group of three or four people talking: the medium shot would establish the group before the camera moved in to a closer shot of whichever character you wanted to feature at that moment.

The shot we used, MEDIUM CLOSE, takes in most of Thorpe's body. It is close enough for us to see his features, but far enough back to include some books and the window, to suggest the kind of room we are in. When you write a sustained scene involving two characters, they should be in a medium close shot most of the time.

Incidentally, CAMERA ANGLE WIDENS means simply that the camera moves slightly (probably to the back and to the side), just enough to permit us to see Sylvia's entrance.

Next in the scale comes the CLOSE SHOT. This shows Thorpe from the waist up, and we get a very good look at him. We see only a fraction of background, probably not enough to identify it. However, there is enough room in a close shot for us to depict two people close together, if we want to; this is what is meant by CLOSE TWO SHOT, frequently used for scenes between two people.

Now we come to CLOSE-UP, a term you surely know. In a close-up a person's face fills the entire screen. (A close-up usually refers to a character, not a thing. Correct terminology for an inanimate object that fills the screen—a ring of keys, say, or a diamond ring, or a letter that must be legible to the spectator—is INSERT.) Close-ups should be employed sparingly, and always for good reason. Write CLOSE-UP in your script if you want to show an important reaction by a character, or if what he is saying is vital. A close-up is for emphasis: it is not to be tossed in arbitrarily because you have written two whole pages without a camera break, and you think one of those directions in capitals would look nice on the page. (But in 1928 Carl Dreyer, the Danish genius of the cinema, made the experimental *Passion of Joan of Arc,* a memorable film shot almost entirely in close-ups. In movies you can always find an exception to a rule, if you hunt.)

This is about the extent of your camera headings, except for two refinements you will use from time to time. These are the POV SHOT (for point of view) and the REVERSE ANGLE. You write in POV SHOT when you want to show what a character sees. Suppose we are back in Thorpe's library, and Thorpe and Sylvia are talking together in a medium close shot. Over the shot comes the sound of the library door opening. Thorpe and Sylvia stop talking, and look off to see who has opened the door. Now we cut to the door, and see what they see, a small child, let's say, photographed in a medium shot. This shot of the child will be headed POV SHOT or simply WHAT THEY SEE (presumably followed by a detailed direction.)

A REVERSE ANGLE is just that: your subject is seen from the reverse point of view. For instance: in one shot a character has his back to us (to the camera). In the next shot we are looking at his face; the camera is photographing him from the reverse of its position in the previous shot. So—REVERSE ANGLE.

Getting Started

I have two suggestions if you want to make a knowledge of these camera terms second nature.

First, take the examples in this chapter and expand them. I suspect that merely memorizing the names of the shots is a waste of time. *Work* with them.

Go back to that Iowa street, and write a scene between the two people we saw driving towards us in the wagon. What they say to each other is unimportant right now. For that scene—which will follow immediately the establishing long shot we opened with—go to a medium close shot (or a close shot) of the boy and girl on the front seat of the wagon.

Get used to writing dialogue. Make sure that your directions are clear, written interestingly (for the benefit of the producer and director), and no fuller than necessary. Don't be carried away. The audience, remember, will not read them.

Or you might take the scene between Arnold and Grace. Backtrack to the point where the police officer must have come in. What has Arnold done? How does the officer trap him? Write a couple of pages leading up to that fade out, and use three or four different camera shots in the course of showing what the three characters do and say.

Then try your hand at continuing that other sequence in Thorpe's library. Show how Sylvia reacts to Thorpe's gratuitous insult, and dramatize the scene that follows. Its *shape* might be something like this: a medium close shot of both of them. Then a close-up of Sylvia as she says something significant, followed by a close-up of Thorpe as he reacts (pained? angry? amused?) to her words. Then a close shot, with both of them in it, to bring your sequence to its conclusion.

Calling the Shots

The second exercise will provide a change of pace. Turn on your television set and watch a dramatic program. An old movie will do. It should be something you don't think you'll like, so you won't become engrossed. I am not being facetious: this is a chore that requires detachment. Name each *kind* of scene as it appears on the screen, together with the transitions between the scenes: long shot, medium, medium close, close-up, dissolve, and so forth.

Try doing this with a friend or colleague—someone from your class, perhaps. You can check each other, disagree as to the nature of certain shots, argue and discuss. The process can not only be painless, it can be positively entertaining.

It may occur to you, as you watch, that I have not yet mentioned the transition from one shot to the next which occurs most frequently in a picture. This is the cut, the instantaneous scene change. You "cut" from a long shot to a medium shot within a sequence; you "cut" from a close-up of a girl screaming to a close-up of a man wondering what's wrong with her.

But in writing your teleplay it is not necessary to spell out this most common of directions. The convention is that when one scene follows another in a script, *without* any specific direction between the shots, it is a cut.

A cut means going directly from a scene on one frame of film to a different scene (or shot or angle) on the next frame. And since these frames are projected on the screen at the rate of several hundred a minute, a cut is the quickest way to get where you're going. It is literally as quick as a wink. When I was producing *Lawman,* a half-hour television series, I worked with one very talented writer who would be swept away when he was writing an exciting scene, full of action. He used to write FAST CUT TO as a direction between his shots. If you are ever similarly tempted, stop and try to figure out what a SLOW CUT would be . . . .

The Inevitable Exception

There is an exception to this rule of not writing CUT TO before a direction. It is a style of picture making which dispenses with dissolves and fades and, for dramatic effect, cuts (goes instantly) from one sequence to another with no regard for time or space. For example:

You are writing a dramatic scene, set in the office of the district attorney. It rises to a climax when the district attorney says grimly to his aides: "There's just one question, gentlemen, I'm going to ask him in cross-examination tomorrow. That question will send him to the gas chamber!"

Now—you want to keep up this suspense, this tension; you don't want the slightest interruption in the swift onrush of your story. You cut—instantaneous transition—to a courtroom miles away, twenty-four hours later. You pick up the district attorney in the middle of his cross examination. The first line he speaks phrases that question we heard mentioned only seconds before. When you use this kind of cut for effect—we might call it a shock cut—then indicate it in your teleplay. Write CUT TO between the scenes that are really far apart in time and space. It will avoid confusion, and will save your producer the trouble of going back to see if he missed something or if you forgot to put in a dissolve.

This technique of the shock cut seems to have originated with the young French directors of the 1950's who adopted a radical, experimental approach towards film-making. The movement was known as the New Wave, and some of its characteristics (like the shock cut) were seized on by American movie producers and also influenced our television. There is no denying the effectiveness of the device when it is properly used. It gives urgency, a feeling of breathless speed, to sequences of crisis. Its indiscriminate use, without regard to the pace or content of your story, can be tiresome. This was vividly demonstrated a few years ago when many pictures dispensed entirely with dissolves and fades and told their stories solely in cuts. Today's trend is visibly back to orthodoxy.

So Much for Grammar

Those are the principal things you should know about teleplay technique. The terms we have examined—shots, dissolves, cuts, and so forth—and the manner in which they are used in the television script constitute the grammar of the teleplay. This grammar, remember, is also the grammar of the screenplay, the much longer script for the motion picture that is designed to be shown in theaters rather than on television screens. The technical terminology you employ for filmed television is the same, without exception, that you would use in writing a theatrical screenplay.

This survey of our teleplay grammar is reasonably complete. There are a few elements we haven't yet covered and which we shall take up in Chapter IV. But that's enough for the time being. We don't want to make the subject seem difficult when it's really not, or to give you mental indigestion by feeding you too much at the outset. Later on we shall learn about such things as the proper movement of the camera, some of the intricacies of directing a telefilm, and the writer's relationship with the director.

For the present, enough of how you set about writing a teleplay. It is time to consider a much more important subject: what you write.

II

The Mechanics of Creation

Plot is a word with derogatory connotations. Like an old live oak, it has become draped with Spanish moss. Such parasitic associations as "artificial," "contrived," and "mechanical" enfeeble it. This is a pity, because *plot,* defined by the dictionary as "a plan of action for a story," is a convenient term. And every television play has one.

It is not important whether you call your play structure a plot, a scheme, a scenario, narrative line, or just plain story. What is of overwhelming importance is how you go about obtaining it. If you think in terms of story gimmicks and twists and sure-fire plot ideas, you will, barring miracles, come up with the kind of plot that has discredited the word.

The nineteenth century melodrama, known to students of the theater as the "well-made play," is an instance of this. All too often, wrote the critic William Archer, the well made play was an ill made play. It was competently carpentered, in the sense that it had a beginning, a middle, and an end, but it abounded in unlikely situations, unexpected surprises, and unbelievable scenes. It was ill made because its people were puppets instead of rounded, thoughtfully drawn characters. The author cared insufficiently for his creatures' natures and personalities; he relied on taking them through a series of ingenious and exciting plot developments to keep his theater filled.

Today's audiences are more sophisticated. The shows that draw crowded houses and high television ratings excel in character portrayal. They have engrossing plot developments, too, but first and foremost they are about people of bone and sinew, not marionettes with flexible joints. Character is basic.

A truism, found in so many books on dramatic technique that it has attained the respectable status of a cliché, proclaims "Plot is character in action."

This emphasis on character is, of course, familiar to those of you who have studied fiction writing and who have written short stories. Perhaps you have written stories that are all character probing and no plot. Television does not permit this indulgence: you will be dealing with stories that have in common a beginning, a middle, and an end, that are composed of a series of situations. But you will be under the same compulsion to draw dimensional, flesh-and-blood people. Before we can care about the things that are happening on our television screen, we have to care about the people they are happening to.

The Very Beginning

Everybody agrees character is basic. It's like being in favor of virtue. But how do you get started? What's the procedure—the very first step?

You might commence by thinking of a character, possibly one resembling a person you know. Visualize this figure. Explore him. Know him. Invent a situation to challenge him. Ask yourself how, with the attributes you have given him, he will react to this situation. Perhaps he will seek help and advice from someone to cope with his predicament, and that someone, his traits and personality also explored and realized, becomes your second character. This second one may have strong views opposed to those held by the first person, and out of this comes a dramatic conflict between two characters.

Certain authorities on dramatic writing insist that this approach to the creation of a dramatic story is actually the dialectics of Hegel's philosophy. You begin with a thesis, confront it with its antithesis, and their clash results in another development: synthesis. But the synthesis, now a higher thesis, also collides with its antithesis and out of this comes a still higher synthesis, and so we spiral upward to our play's denouement. It is only fair to point out that other authorities, equally qualified, regard this interpretation as unnecessary pedantry.

Another way to begin. Create several characters, bearing some relation to each other. Perhaps they all live in the same New York tenement, or they're together in the trenches on the Somme in 1916, or they are all prisoners in Sing Sing. Think about these characters, add to them, before you give a thought to the situation in which you eventually propose to involve them. See what happens as you put them down on paper and bring them to life. From them will come at least one idea (probably two or three) for a story subject. The late Kenneth Macgowan, when he was chairman of the Theater Arts Department at the University of California at Los Angeles, told of once seeing a pupil's play take form from just such a mere description of a set of characters, because they were so vivid and—suggested as they were by the playwright's own experience—so well observed.

Nobody can tell you *exactly* how to begin any more than he can write your story for you. You are an embryo playwright, not a stenographer. But it is permissible to give a detailed illustration, a variation of the first approach to this awesome business of creation, expressed in concrete terms.

I'll begin by thinking of two characters, a man named Richard and another one named Robin. Richard is a successful, respected citizen who lives his life according to the rules and the ideals of the society to which he belongs. He follows high standards, tends to be rigid, and believes there is a correct answer to any question fate poses him. I think in visual terms. I give him behavior which visibly relates to the kind of person he is. I show him being impatient with a colleague who doesn't act as Richard believes he should. I want Robin to have a different character; I start building him as a contrast to Richard, charming, somewhat irresponsible, impulsive, a bit of a ne'er-do-well. But I'd like him to have humor and compassion, qualities not immediately perceptible in Richard. Already a conflict is taking shape. What happens when an exciting situation arises to test their respective characters? Shall I take the path of least resistance, and show Robin, with his adaptability and essential goodness, coming out victorious over rigid Richard? Or do I avoid the expected, and probe deeper into their characters, which might lead me to a conclusion vindicating Richard, whose principles solve a problem that swamps Robin's charming, easygoing nature? In all likelihood other people are involved in this situation, this problem that must be solved. Is one of these people a girl? Are both men in love with her? Is she Richard's wife? And what's my setting for this story, anyhow? A big business office with a power struggle going on between rival executives? A mining camp on the Sacramento? A Democratic presidential convention in Milwaukee? Scott's dash for the South Pole?

You can't deny possibilities are opening up. And they all arise from the two characters with whom I arbitrarily started. Answer the kind of question they inevitably pose, according to your own taste, and you are well along to constructing a plot from character.

Confusing Commandments

Probably a hundred books on how to write for the theater have appeared in this country since George Pierce Baker published *Dramatic Technique* in 1919. You can learn a great deal from these books; you can also become thoroughly confused, because authorities disagree violently on certain rules. One school insists a playwright must have a theme before he dare even dream about his characters or their function. Lajos Egri holds that the theme of *Macbeth* is "Ruthless ambition leads to its own destruction," just as the theme of Sean O'Casey's *Juno and the Paycock* is "Shiftlessness leads to ruin." (Myself, I would have thought *Juno's* theme, if it has one, was to be found in Captain Boyle's view of things: "The worl' is in a state o' chassis.") But another school, also deserving respect and attention, contends that any such rule about a play's thesis puts the cart before the horse. Certainly a play has a thesis, say these pundits, but you do not first think of a theme and then fit your characters and action into it. The theme develops as you go along, it emerges as the play is written, and sometimes the theme is not fully apparent to the author until he has written "Finis."

There are other theories, expanded by some into laws, opposed or just ignored by others.

Fortunately, we are not in such a state of "chassis" as the foregoing might indicate. There are certain rules that all authorities subscribe to. These rules are the important ones. The squabbles seem to boil up over peripheral notions, imaginative refinements of the major laws that govern writing in the dramatic forms. The rules we will learn to observe in this chapter belong to the noncontroversial order. They are guides, signposts set up with academic approval, and I have found them valid in practice, in writing and producing motion pictures for television. Naturally, we won't be concerned with rules that apply only to the stage. We will concentrate on those which govern the television medium.

We have already explored, tentatively, the first precept—the importance of character in starting to invent your story. If we go deeper into the subject, the resulting discussion leads inevitably to consideration of additional tested ways and means to construct a teleplay.

You noticed one thing right away about the two characters I used in my suggested first step in devising a story. Robin and Richard are in conflict. They are two different breeds of cat. When they come together, under circumstances of stress and tension, there is bound to be an explosion.

The Importance of Disagreement

It is possible to generalize from this specific. Characters whose personalities are in opposition provide conflict, and conflict of some sort is a primary element of your teleplay. It goes without saying (a deceptive phrase, meaning "This is important") that the characters must be interesting. A pair of dullards can be in bitter conflict and bore us to death. Your men and women must be interesting, and they must react on each other. A group of bland people, in agreement with each other and their neighbors, makes for happy family life but dull drama.

At the beginning, then, the writer deals with these factors: (1) interesting characters who, (2) because of personality differences, react to each other; (3) conflict, physical or psychological, bursts from their reactions; (4) and out of this conflict, this clash, is born the subject, the main situation, the *plot* of your teleplay.

Now these things, when you start putting them down on paper, are unlikely to occur in that strict 1-2-3-4 sequence. You will find yourself juggling two or more of them at once. Immediately after you FADE IN, two of your characters may be found arguing violently about a situation which threatens them. But that opening scene will take shape in a more-or-less complex form *after* you have done your preliminary character-conflict-situation planning.

If you do begin with a scene like this, you will be working within an ancient tradition of drama that dates back to the Greeks: opening "in the middle of things." And starting with an event already in progress is highly desirable in television. You must interest your viewers as quickly as possible. Remember: in this medium you are not writing for a captive audience. In the theater the audience has paid for its seats; it is inclined to be patient if the play or movie it has paid to watch unfolds slowly for the first fifteen minutes, taking time to establish characters and atmosphere. But the television audience can afford to be capricious (at the moment we are not considering pay television). If his interest isn't aroused in a hurry, a viewer can all too easily switch to another channel or turn off the set. Commercial television has long been aware of this peril, and most dramatic or comedy programs begin with a brief, compelling scene, a "teaser" designed to "hook" the audience before the opening titles and commercial come on the screen. I advise you not to begin your teleplay with a gentle, extended pastoral sequence, showing a shepherd boy idly watching his flock. Not unless sheep thieves are in the neighborhood.

Establishing Interest

But you don't have to be lurid about it. You could begin with two of your people speculating about a third character whom they are expecting. What they have to say about him intrigues us. At scene's end we want to see this stranger who will shortly make his appearance.

A recent television picture faded in on the arrival of a wealthy patient in a big hospital. He was a distinguished man of letters and his advent caused commotion. The head of the hospital summoned a member of his staff to ask him what was wrong with the newcomer. Nothing. The writer was in perfect health. Then why on earth was he demanding admission as a patient? Because he insisted that he would be dead within a week.

Then there is the placid (but brief) opening in which nothing untoward happens until the end of the scene when there is a shock stinger. I once wrote an opening sequence that introduced a mild professor and his wife finishing their breakfast. If he didn't hurry he would be late for his economics lecture. He picked up his briefcase, kissed his wife, and was starting out the door when he stopped short and rushed to his study for something he had forgotten. The "something" turned out to be a loaded automatic. He tucked it into his briefcase and hurried off to catch his bus.

There are many ways to write this first scene. It can be a short prologue to your story proper. It can be the first part of an extended scene, a scene that might be played without any interruption at all, if the television program on which your story is seen should not call for a break so early in the unreeling. (But there must be a dramatic moment at which you can interrupt.)

Be sure you don't wrench your story out of shape, just to have a startling opening. It doesn't have to be startling. It can be, of course, but all it *has* to do is interest your audience.

The opening is a promise of entertainment to come—valid because this promise itself is entertaining.

A Look at Strategy

Before we continue with the study of further tactics in this campaign to master a teleplay, let us understand what the over-all strategy is.

It is simply to involve your audience with your characters.

The doctors of the drama have formulated this dictum in many various ways: audiences must *identify* with the characters, they must *worry* about what's happening to them, they must *love* and *hate* the characters, they must be *entertained* by them. The academicians are all saying the same thing we said at the beginning of this chapter: before you can care about a story's happenings, you must care about the people they are happening to. This is why we begin inventing our stories by thinking of characters first and foremost, why we continue to think of them as our stories take shape. A good commander never forgets strategy while he is working out tactics.

Your audience must take sides in the conflict raging between your characters. The audience must be partisan. Their sympathies must be roused and sustained. Detachment on a spectator's part must be avoided at all costs. A disinterested audience is an uninterested audience.

It is manifestly nonsense to suppose that our audience will be instantly absorbed in our people right after FADE IN. Involving our spectators is a process that calls for skill and sincerity because you must be devoted to your characters yourself before you can hope that anyone else will be. Our aim is to make the public more interested in our people at the end of the first act than they were at the beginning, more concerned with their fates at a midway point than they were as the first act ended, and utterly involved as the climax looms up.

The keyword is *growth.* From the moment you introduce your characters, the story must grow. Problems pile up, complications arise, new people come on scene: the growth continues inexorably. It doesn't stop until Arnold goes off to jail for sixty days, or Sylvia confesses her love for the acidulous Thorpe, or Holmes sends Professor Moriarty ("the Napoleon of crime, Watson") plummeting into the Reichenbach Falls.

Do not confuse growth with tempo. Growth should be a constant process in the teleplay. The tempo or pace of your story, except in rare instances, is inconstant: it fluctuates. A scene full of action, moving very rapidly, may be succeeded by a slower one, even a reflective interlude. The expert melodrama may appear to start out at a deliberate pace and accelerate evenly until the suspenseful finish, but this impression is often not valid. If you examine the plot structure, you will notice that the breakneck operation of robbing the Bank of England is immediately followed by a long sequence in which the outlaws remain hidden in a lonely manor house, reacting variously to the pressure of the hunt as the personalities their creator has given them dictate. Yet because the story steadily grows, you are as absorbed in this tense if static scene as you were in the razzle-dazzle that went before.

Characters in Crisis

A story is simply a pattern in which characters move through a series of happenings. A good story is one in which the happenings are increasingly interesting. It grows from the first small happening that presages the bigger happenings to come. Many writers on the drama like to use the word "crisis" to drive home their point that the happenings through which a story progresses are neither bland nor commonplace.

A crisis can be small or large. A crisis is Thomas Becket, cloaked in the Archbishop's authority, turning against his king; it is ten people in a frontier tavern at the moment they realize they are trapped by a flood; it is Scarlett O'Hara vowing she will never be hungry again; and it is a small boy who goes out in the back yard and finds that his dog has run away. A crisis is not necessarily a cataclysm; it can be something so unremarkable as to be of importance only to the person who is experiencing this happening, something to go unnoticed by an indifferent spectator. But we the audience are not indifferent spectators: we are identifying with the character we are watching, and therefore the crisis important to him is important to us . . . unless you the writer have botched your story.

The biggest crisis of all occurs just before the finish of your teleplay, and it is, of course, the climax. It can be violent or restrained, dramatic, terrifying, uproarious, tragic; but the one thing all climaxes have to be is satisfying. It is what the audience, consciously or not, *wants* to happen. Looking back on the play, the spectator should feel that this biggest crisis of all was inevitable. It is the thing that supremely "should have happened."

All this talk of violence and restraint, floods and Thomas Becket, may give the impression that I am exclusively concerned with drama and melodrama. Not so. Everything in this chapter applies to comedy as well. If you ignore those rules about character and conflict, you will produce a silly, inane farce instead of the hilarious piece you hope you're writing. Crisis is comedy's life blood, too. When Lord Babington is persuaded to impersonate Charley's aunt from Brazil, it's a crisis. It's a bigger one when the real aunt shows up. The climax (biggest crisis) of *The School for Scandal* is the discovery of Lady Teazle hiding behind the screen.

These rules for writing a television script come to us from Aeschylus and Sophocles, from Molière, Shakespeare, Shaw, and David Wark Griffith. From *Oedipus* to *Saint Joan,* the plays alive today observed the principles of character, conflict, and crisis. And of the Three C's the greatest of all is character.

The Theater of Convention

The time we live in has been seeing a revolution in the drama. We are moving away from the Theater of Reality (true-to-life naturalistic representation) towards our own version of the Theater of Convention, which offers greater freedom of action, and greater freedom in the expression of ideas.

There is nothing new about the Theater of Convention. It has existed at many periods in many parts of the world. It might also be termed the Theater of Convenience because its essence is the use of nonrealistic conveniences to reveal events with speed and economy. The ritual pattern of the centuries-old but still existent Japanese Nō plays, in which a character's stylized gesture can reveal his identity and something of his history, belongs to the Theater of Convention. So does the Greek chorus which, standing aloof from the actors, comments on and explains the action of the story. The language of Shakespeare and the Elizabethan platform performances of his plays illustrate this time-honored approach to the drama, too.

Most of the western world in the nineteenth century, however, became used to the play that mirrored events as faithfully and realistically as possible, a tradition that is still vigorous today and dominant in motion pictures and television. The Theater of Convention does not try to imitate life: it forces its audiences to accept *conventions* as story-telling devices. In 1937 Thornton Wilder's chronicle of a New Hampshire town used a bare stage and a critic-narrator, and ignored reality as the dead mingled with the living in *Our Town* and people climbed ladders to represent going upstairs in their houses. The devices of the Theater of Convention enable the playwright to include much that the limitations of the Theater of Reality make impractical. Time is telescoped: if *Our Town* were rewritten in naturalistic terms, it would probably take three nights to perform. In the later *The Skin of Our Teeth* Wilder symbolically identified one family with the entire human race to present the story of mankind. More recently we have had the extremely unlifelike innovations of the Theater of the Absurd.

Do not think that this is a movement peculiar to one section of the theater, that it is something separate from television. It has influenced television indirectly (the shock cuts that annihilate needless narrative), but directly, too. We have seen Samuel Beckett's *Waiting for Godot* on television. In England, many avant garde playwrights are working in the medium of commercial television, notably Harold

Pinter, whose contradictory, dreamlike *The Lover* won an Oscar (British) as the best original television drama of its year.

But the fascinating point is that these far-out plays also need and use the drama's birthright of character, conflict, crisis, and the growth process. The people of Ionesco's *Rhinoceros* face a mounting nightmare (crisis after crisis) as they transform themselves into the giant horned mammals symbolizing brute conformity. The weird but dimensional tramps, Estragon and Vladimir, of Beckett's religious allegory, *Waiting for Godot,* are in perpetual conflict as they keep their fruitless vigil. *Godot* begins in obscurity and ends in mystery, but it attains its goal through a series of mad crises. Even Beckett's most exasperating play, *Happy Days,* has something of the obligatory pattern. Its principal character is buried to her waist in earth during the first act. But as her attempts to communicate continue, during this dotty examination of the human condition, the next act finds her up to her neck. She is worse off. It's crisis. It's growth.

The rules, then, seem to work for Genet and Max Frisch as they did for Sophocles and Euripides. I doubt if you can improve on them.

The Customary Three Acts

Nothing compels you to think of your story in terms of three acts, but you will find it useful to do so. Dramatic pieces divide rather naturally into thirds. There is usually a major crisis at the end of the first act, a bigger one at the end of the second, and a climax in the third, followed by the resolution. These elements may shift around a bit—maybe the second act curtain is your climax—and you are perfectly free so to shift them.

Until fifty years ago, most plays had four or five acts. Nevertheless, study the plot outlines of Ibsen's *Hedda Gabler,* Veiller's *Within the Law,* or Pinero's *The Second Mrs. Tanqueray,* and you will find that they divide roughly into three segments. When one of the old-timers is revived today, it is customary to present the five acts as three: the first act may now have two scenes (formerly acts one and two); the second act will be what was formerly the third; and the modern act three will consist of the old fourth and fifth acts as scenes one and two. Seldom is there a sense of violence done the original structure.

We tend to think of a half-hour television drama as the equivalent of a one-act play. But even a one-act play often breaks into three parts.

Let me summarize for you a melodrama called *Tunnel of Fear,* a half-hour film with David Niven and Cedric Hardwicke playing the two leads. It was shown on the anthology program *Four Star Playhouse,* and it illustrates all the rules we have been talking about. It illustrates them in simple, actually primitive, form. This teleplay had only two characters of any importance, and most of the story occurred as they talked to each other in the compartment of an English train. The ancient unities of time, place, and action were observed here with a vengeance.

The picture fades in at a country railroad station where a prosperous-looking gentleman (Hardwicke) is being carried aboard a train. He is obviously unable to walk. As his servants lift him into his private compartment, we cut to a seedy, suspicious-looking stranger, lurking behind a post, and watching intently. Niven is the sinister fellow.

(Now—two characters are established immediately. They rouse our interest. Why is one man being carried? Why is the shabby stranger so intently watching the first man?)

From a brief conversation between the rich man and his servants, as they make him comfortable in his private compartment, we learn that Sir Henry is crippled by arthritis, that in spite of this he travels alone up to London once a week to look after business interests, and that secretaries meet him there to take him to his office. As the servants leave the train, and Sir Henry settles down to read his copy of the *Times,* we cut outside to the platform. The train starts to move; the stranger scuttles across the platform from his hiding place and leaps aboard. A moment later, he enters Sir Henry's compartment without knocking. Sir Henry politely protests this invasion of his privacy, but the seedy one merely smiles impudently and sits down.

(This is the end of our first scene. There is a break here for the commercial. Afterwards, the action picks up without any time lapse. The obligation to intrigue our audience at once has been fulfilled. The stranger's invasion of the compartment is the first *crisis.* And there is every promise of *conflict* to come.)

Ignoring Sir Henry's protests, the stranger chatters away with offensive familiarity. He knows about Sir Henry, referring to him scoffingly as one of the wealthiest and most respected men in all

England. As the stranger comments sneeringly on Sir Henry's philanthropies, the crippled man reaches for the buzzer to summon the conductor. The other roughly pushes him away, then lowers the blinds on the inner door of the compartment leading to the train aisle.

(The action is heightened by another, bigger crisis.)

Menacingly, the stranger asks Sir Henry if he doesn't remember him. They used to be good friends. Sir Henry denies ever having seen him before.

"It's been twenty years, Henry," says the stranger, "and I've changed. But you'll remember the name: Jerry Morgan."

Stunned, Sir Henry sinks back, staring. We know by his expression that he does recognize Jerry Morgan.

(A crisis brings the first third of the story to its end. The conflict that began with the baiting of the helpless man has continued to rise. The reasons for the conflict are beginning to take shape.)

The tense dialogue that follows reveals the relationship between Sir Henry and Jerry Morgan. Twenty years before, penniless adventurers in South Africa, they robbed a diamond cache, planning to split the loot. Because Henry deserted him, Jerry was caught and did twenty years in prison. His partner got away free with the diamonds, used them to found his fortune and position—while Jerry Morgan rotted in jail. Now Jerry is free, and his only purpose in life is to settle the score with the man who left him in the lurch.

A frightened man, Sir Henry tries to excuse his running out. As restitution, he offers to make Jerry wealthy. Jerry plays cat-and-mouse with the helpless man. He affects to weigh Sir Henry's offer. Then, suddenly breaking off, he tells how he has studied the other's moves for weeks. He knows how Sir Henry takes this train to London every week. He has memorized the route and schedule. In a few minutes the train will enter a tunnel. When it emerges, it always slows down, and that is when Jerry will jump off. Why? To make good his escape. While the train is in the blackness of the tunnel, Jerry is going to kill Sir Henry.

(This is the end of our miniature second act. The threat to Sir Henry, implicit from the moment of Jerry's entrance, is finally articulated. Our second part finishes with the biggest crisis so far. We are still promising more to come; we are not permitting the audience to relax.)

Sir Henry struggles for composure. He does not plead for his life. Instead, he puts up a powerful argument. He pictures the hangman's rope that waits for Jerry. Then, altering tactics, he says he knows Jerry. Knows his nature. Knows that, whatever the circumstances, Jerry is not able to kill in cold blood. Jerry is visibly shaken.

(This is growth in terms of character. Conflict reaches a higher pitch, as Sir Henry, hitherto helpless and fearful, finds courage to fight back.)

Jerry pulls himself together. He implacably repeats his intention. He has lived for twenty years with the thought of this moment to sustain him: the moment of revenge.

But Sir Henry appears to have derived inner strength from his conviction that Jerry cannot, will not, kill. His self-possession infuriates the other. As the train enters the tunnel, Jerry pulls a knife from his pocket, and starts towards Sir Henry. The last thing we see before the blackness of the tunnel engulfs the screen is a close-up of Sir Henry's horrified face.

(The biggest crisis of all. The climax.)

The train comes out of the tunnel. Jerry is back in his seat, defeated. He looks at the knife, still in his hand, then thrusts it back in his pocket. He admits quietly that he could not go through with it. He *is* unable to take a life. Henry is right. Henry knows him better than he knows himself.

He looks questioningly at Sir Henry. Sir Henry stares back with sightless eyes. Jerry, in mounting terror, reaches for him. Sir Henry falls over. He is quite dead. Livid, Jerry tries to revive him. Useless. Terror stopped Sir Henry's heart, and Jerry is a murderer in spite of himself. He literally frightened his old enemy to death. His face contorted with remorse and anguish, Jerry presses the buzzer.

(What happens when the train comes out of the tunnel is your denouement, the resolution of your story. It is about the most compact example of a resolution that I have even seen.)

The Mortar for the Bricks

In the next chapter I want to talk about the final major ingredient of dramatic writing. It is preparation. It is the most important of all, because it embraces all the others—character, conflict, crisis, growth.

It is simply the art of making credible the series of events that advance your story; of persuading your audience to believe and accept the shocks and surprises, big and little, you have in store for them. Without this artful preparation, character is contradictory, conflict is bewildering, crisis is ludicrous.

In the meantime, I suggest you select certain portions of my synopsis of *Tunnel of Fear* and dramatize them, with full directions and dialogue. Bear in mind that although this is a kind of Grand Guignol shocker, its suspense comes out of the characters of the two men. One has made himself wealthy and powerful, building his eminently respectable life on a crime; he has resources of strength that determine his attitude towards his opponent, a desperate man who has spent twenty years of misery with only the thought of vengeance to sustain him. Their characters, moulded by these backgrounds, provide you with the key to what they say and how they act.

If your zeal and energy go beyond the call of duty, write a thirty-page teleplay that tells the entire story.

III

The Art of Preparation

"A startling idea must not be sprung upon an audience wholly unprepared to accept it."

This is the nutshell into which the whole theory of dramatic preparation was put by William Archer over half a century ago. He was echoing the rule formulated fifty years before *that*, by the younger Dumas, the most successful playwright of his generation. Few playwrights in the last hundred years have violated the practice. (If you perversely hunt for exceptions, you will, of course, come across Gilbert and Sullivan's *Pinafore* and *Gondoliers*, in each of which Sir William Gilbert devised for his climax the preposterous revelation that certain people had been switched in their cradles as babies, and were not who they seemed to be. The audience, grossly unprepared for these last-minute surprises, never objects, since the outrageous denouements are a deliberate part of the fun.) The worldly authors of the "well made play," who prided themselves on solid plot construction no matter how improbable its elements, minded the necessity for preparation. One of the most successful said, in effect: "If you're going to sink the ship in the last act, you must first let the audience know that the vessel is leaky, and then later inform them that a storm is approaching."

Today preparation is usually focused on character. Is the action of the person we are watching on the television screen believable in the light of his personality and behavior, as revealed to us before that action? Is Winifred's saintly act of sacrifice in the last five minutes of the picture consistent with her personality as we have seen it exposed throughout the story?

Let us look at some famous crisis scenes:

1. An aging chiropractor, discovering that a young girl who boards with him and his wife is having an affair with an athlete, reacts by drinking himself blind and attacking his wife with a hatchet.
2. A wealthy southern woman of 1900 impassively watches her husband die of a heart attack, refusing to fetch from a nearby room the medicine which could save his life.
3. A migratory farm worker fondles a young woman and, when she becomes frightened, unintentionally breaks her neck.
4. A self-assured naval officer, disciplined and imposing, quickly turns into a quivering, nervous wreck when he is cross-examined on the witness stand.

Summarized baldly, these incidents are unbelievable. But they are not unbelievable in their respective contexts: they are inevitable. We believe them, we accept them, so thoroughly has the depiction of each character prepared us for his reactions to a given situation. By the time the dread crisis is reached, we feel we know the character, we have seen his conduct in a number of relationships; although we may be appalled and shocked by what he does at the crucial moment, we are receptive, we understand.

A Closer Look at Crisis

Before "Doc" takes the hatchet to his slatternly wife in William Inge's *Come Back, Little Sheba,* he has been revealed to us as a deeply troubled man, a chronic drunkard maintaining a precarious hold on sobriety through the fellowship of Alcoholics Anonymous. We have seen his great affection for the beautiful child who rents a room in their ramshackle home, his belief in her innocence. We know that Doc has a partially hidden resentment towards Lola, his incessantly chattering spouse, a resentment that will take who knows what form if ever he hits the bottle again. When Doc makes his shattering discovery that the girl, his daughter-image, has spent the night with a boy whom he detests and whom he has asked his wife to bar from the house, we dread what will happen. We are afraid he will start drinking. Our fears are confirmed. We anticipate the explosion. When it comes, it unnerves us. Its impact is staggering because we believe it. We "knew" something like this would happen. We have been *prepared.*

The woman who watches her husband die in the second illustration is Regina Giddens, the avaricious anti-heroine of *The Little Foxes* by Lillian Hellman. Her behavior is that of a monster—if you will accept as the definition of monster a human who is so unfeeling, so crafty and calculating, so determined to gratify self, and so utterly ruthless that you can believe she will commit any enormity to get what she wants. These are the qualities in the character Miss Hellman painstakingly created through two and a half acts, convincing us by means of brilliant, distressing detail that Regina is a woman impervious to compassion, contemptuous of decency, capable of anything. When Horace Giddens gasps out his life before Regina's eyes, we are held in terrible fascination because—once again—we believe it, we have been prepared for it.

In *Of Mice and Men* John Steinbeck gave us a character in the amiable but dangerous Lennie whose doom is shadowed from the play's beginning. Lennie is a feeble-minded giant of enormous strength. His friend, George, takes care of him. Without George, we feel, Lennie would not be able to exist. In this case, the preparation for the penultimate happening is carried out on an elementary level. We know that Lennie likes to stroke small animals, and we have seen his dismay when his powerful hands crush them to death. We also know that Lennie got into trouble and had to flee when he terrified a girl by trying to stroke her dress. These two pieces of knowledge combine to prepare us for the crisis when the daughter-in-law of Lennie's boss tempts him into stroking her hair. The woman suddenly becomes frightened and screams, and Lennie, trying to quiet her, breaks her neck.

When the commanding officer of the *USS Caine* first testifies on the witness stand in Herman Wouk's *The Caine Mutiny Court Martial,* Lieutenant Commander Queeg is correct, self-assured, and conducts himself as admirably as we feel a naval officer should. But when the defence counsel for the mutinous officers recalls Queeg to the stand and subjects him to relentless pressure, the martinet suddenly cracks under the strain and degenerates into a pitiable man on the brink of madness. We are shaken but far from incredulous: we have had the account of Queeg's aberrations indicating his neurasthenic condition.

We are moved and discomfited by his extraordinary antics, but by no means flabbergasted.

You will need to exercise all your skill in this business of preparation; otherwise you will give away too much too soon. A familiar admonition in the argot of movies and television is: "Don't telegraph your punches." Don't be so intent on your preparation that you let your audience know exactly what is going to happen. There is, obviously, a fine line between telling them just enough so they will accept your climax and telling them too much. A most important part of your craft is learning where to draw this line. We have all seen poorly constructed television shows in which we could guess what was going to happen after watching ten minutes of the picture. We lost interest because there was no real suspense, and we probably switched channels. There is a strong probability that the author of the telefilm which telegraphed its punches was thinking in terms of plot. It is much more difficult to refrain from telling your audience precisely what you are up to if you insist on using story clues and plot incidents as the elements of your preparation and relegate your characterization to a secondary place.

Read *The Little Foxes* and *Come Back, Little Sheba* and make a note of each subtle character revelation, each incident related to character, designed to prepare us for the climax. Armed with hindsight, you will find many examples that collectively lead you to the conclusion: "Of course—this was bound to happen. Here—and here—and again at the end of the first act." But so artfully have these dramas been constructed that, lacking precognition, you could never guess the *exact* nature of the climactic happening. Miss Hellman and Mr. Inge knew where and how to draw that line.

Exposition

Exposition is sometimes regarded as a part of Preparation. If it is not quite that, it is certainly Preparation's twin. Both give the audience information. Preparation, we have seen, gives them information in the present. Exposition deals with the past: it tells the audience what took place *before* the play or motion picture or television film started.

If you fade in on a family group quarreling over the terms of eccentric old Aunt Eloise's bizarre will, you will probably find it advisable to reveal something, before you get too deeply into your teleplay, about the way Aunt Eloise died, what it was she did that made her eccentric, and the nature of the bequests which have set the loving relatives at each other's throats.

Don't regard exposition as mere carpentry. It is carpentry of a sort, but a very special sort: it requires ingenuity, imagination, the full use of your critical sense, in fact as conscientious an application of your creative powers as you would accord the development of a major character or the building of your teleplay's most important scene. Your object is to work the exposition into your script so that it is natural and unobtrusive. Mere carpentry? It is highly skilled labor. (Infrequently, the words of an unseen narrator—whose voice is heard over a scene that relates to what he is telling us—are used to present the exposition. But narration, a technique borrowed from the documentary or fact film, should be resorted to only in those extremely rare cases when other methods of exposition prove clumsy and ineffective.)

Dramatic literature is full of examples of awkward exposition, most of them to be found in anthologies of old plays that gather dust on library shelves. Years ago the curtain would go up on a society comedy, and we would find ourselves listening to a housemaid and a butler conversing as they went about their tasks. They would tell us (and each other) that young Humphrey Vanderlip had been drinking and carousing again, and that his father was going to send him Out West to make a man of him. This prepared the audience for the entrance of Master Humphrey with a suitcase and a hangover, and the play proper began. When he was a theater critic, Robert Benchley complained about the kind of stodgy historical play that always seemed to open in some royal anteroom where (I quote from memory), at curtain's rise, the Comte de Rochambeau was discovered telling Benjamin Franklin: "As you know, my dear Franklin, this is the year 1789. As you also know, France stands at the dread brink of revolution. You, as the representative of a nation which has but recently won its freedom from England, have been summoned by His Majesty, King Louis XVI, to advise us how we should deal with those demagogues, Danton and Robespierre."

Such devices have long since been laughed out of the theater, but the necessity for exposition is still with us.

We believe we know how to handle it today.

In a certain type of story, you may decide that the best way to present your exposition is by means of a prologue, in which you show the audience what they have to know instead of telling them about it. Well and good, if the exposition makes a dramatic sequence: since you are writing for the motion picture–television medium, you will frequently be able to show instead of tell. But many stories would be ruined by such an approach. Imagine *Tunnel of Fear* beginning with a prologue in which we saw Sir Henry stealing the diamonds and his confederate going to jail, and the next scene coming on with a subtitle saying, "Twenty years later." You would have your exposition, all right, but interest and suspense would have gone down the drain.

Nor, in all likelihood, would it be advisable to start with Aunt Eloise being eccentric, dictating her will, and then succumbing to a thrombosis. In this fragment, and also in *Tunnel,* the exposition, closely related to the characters, can be an absorbing part of the action, not merely "something the audience must know." What happened to Aunt Eloise should be revealed little by little through the words and actions of the characters with whom we will be concerned throughout the teleplay.

Sleight of Hand

Exposition (the prologue is a special case), then, is the art of sliding in vital information, as nearly imperceptibly as possible, while the story moves ahead. What your people say, explanatorily, must seem to be what they would naturally say at a certain time, in a certain place, under certain circumstances.

The audience must never think that your story is stopping while something is being explained to them. "We are being entertained," is what they must feel. Not "We are learning something that will probably turn out to be important." Character and incident and back-story should all be tightly combined. You are slipping something over on your audience—exposition.

Guard against impatience. It is your enemy in any kind of writing, and never deadlier than in this area of dramatic exposition. Novice playwrights tend to be overwhelmed by a false urgency. It is a sense of needing to tell everything in the back-story as soon as possible after the curtain rises or the picture fades in. It's a compulsion: the feeling that you can't really proceed with your story until past history has been taken care of. Resist this obsession; put it out of your mind. The way to present your exposition is to *weave* it into the fabric of your teleplay.

Observe how Tennessee Williams deals with Blanche Dubois's past in *A Streetcar Named Desire*. We know within a few minutes after poor, neurotic Blanche's entrance in the first scene that she is a phoney, but the truth about her lubricious life as a school teacher in Laurel—the full revelation of her character and her tragedy—comes out little by little throughout two-thirds of the play. It is revealed dynamically. We learn about the past while we are absorbed in the present. This stringing out of exposition in *Streetcar* is an extreme example of delayed exposition. You will find a more conventional treatment of exposition in Robert Sherwood's play, *The Petrified Forest,* where we rapidly and painlessly take in the past histories of the motley characters gathered together in the lonely lunchroom in the Arizona desert. Sherwood so deftly inserts his exposition that it combines with present action to push the play forward.

These examples appear to give the lie to *Tunnel of Fear* where the back-story was handed to us in one big solid block. But that teleplay was knowingly devised so we should want the past to be made known in a single revelation. Exposition in the opening scenes was not a means, as usual, but an end. The audience was shown two men who obviously had a relationship; it was made to wonder what that relationship could be. It was teased along, made to *want* the exposition that could throw light on the mystery. The exposition was withheld until curiosity reached a peak and had to be satisfied unless exasperation was to replace it. At that moment the audience was not only ready for but demanding the long explanation which, in a different kind of script, should be avoided.

Complexity

Dirty Hands (*Les Mains sales*), Jean-Paul Sartre's melodrama, brilliantly juggles a mass of exposition in its first scene. In this prologue, the audience must know the history of the leading character—a Communist assassin—and his relations to the party, if they are to understand the events in the long flashback, directly following, that comprises most of the play.

The locale is a small European country in the middle of World War II. At curtain's rise we are in the cottage of Olga, a Communist functionary. Hugo, the assassin hero, appears, having just been released from prison. His advent frightens Olga, but she suppresses her fear. It is soon evident that Hugo, having outlived his usefulness to the party, is going to be liquidated. The execution squad arrives, but Olga wins a reprieve for the condemned man. She undertakes to question Hugo, and determine if he is really a threat to the comrades or whether he can still be used by the party if his life is spared. As he begins to answer Olga's questions, the first scene ends.

As you see, there is a lot of present substance in this eleven-page scene. But Sartre has also set himself the task of explaining the following happenings in the *past:*

The German army has occupied the country where Olga and Hugo live.

The Russians have mounted an offensive, following their victory at Stalingrad.

Olga's country is in the chaotic process of transferring allegiance from Nazi Germany to the USSR.

Hugo has been in prison for some time; he has not escaped, as Olga at first assumes, but was released for good behavior.

He has a wife, Jessica, of whom Olga seems to be jealous. It is hinted that Olga herself loves Hugo.

While Hugo was imprisoned, his Communist superiors, suspecting that the killing he committed was a crime of passion rather than a political act, voted to get rid of him because of political unreliability.

Somebody (Olga, perhaps) sent Hugo a box of poisoned chocolates, but it was his cellmate who ate them and died.

I think you'll agree this is a big packet of information to throw at the audience in the first few minutes of a play. Yet Sartre has treated his exposition so skillfully that we are concerned only with the conflict that is starting up before our eyes. For sheer suspense this opening is the best scene in the play.

Immediately after the curtain rises, a radio Olga has turned on tells us what we have to know of the political background. Olga's alarm when Hugo appears instantly establishes tension. The substance of the scene between them is conflict, veiled at first, then bursting forth. You see, Hugo is perfectly aware of what has been planned for him, and he ironically taunts Olga as she tries to evade his cynical questions about the comrades' plans. The taunting and the response are building character, carrying the story forward, but at the same time laying out the exposition for us. As Olga turns from evasiveness to defiance, the drama heightens. She is torn between party loyalty and her concern for Hugo. By the time Hugo's executioners come in, and Olga temporarily gets rid of them, we have had an intricate background story told us, we understand the situation; we have taken all this in while we were intent on present excitement.

Ibsen's Methods

The greatest playwright of the nineteenth century's last years was the one who always had the most exposition to unload. It has been said of Henrik Ibsen that his plays began at the point where conventional dramas would have closed, that he started with a climax, then devoted his play to what followed the climax. He probed deeper into his characters than any playwright of his time, and because the problems his people faced were so complex, he had much to tell us about the predicaments they found themselves in as his first acts began. A curious footnote to theater history calls attention to the mass of back story in the typical Ibsen play. A forgotten playwright named Austin Fryers, Bernard Shaw tells us, actually wrote and put on the stage the drama which lies implicit in the exposition of *Rosmersholm*. Fryers got a full play out of Ibsen's back-story.

Naturally you should avoid burdening your stories for the television or motion picture mediums with vast quantities of exposition. But Ibsen's technique was usually impeccable, and the mechanics of his plays, still valid today, will repay study.

For Ibsen's plays are no museum pieces. They are very much alive, and they are no strangers to television. Julie Harris has played *A Doll's House* for the little screen, and a televised *Hedda Gabler* starred Ingrid Bergman. The social themes that lent the plays importance in the 1880's and 1890's lack interest now: the vitality is in the powerful personal drama and the admirable construction. Ibsen's construction is still widely used as a model in the teaching of drama writing.

Read (or reread) *Rosmersholm* and *A Doll's House*. Pay attention on every page to their construction, to their character, conflict, crisis, preparation, and exposition. Get hold of a modern English translation: Eva Le Gallienne and Michael Meyer have both done good ones. If you go back to the first great translator of Ibsen, you are likely to be put off by the stilted, old-fashioned language of William Archer's versions. Archer (who introduced Ibsen to Britain and America) was too literal, and he was also influenced by two successful playwrights of his period, Pinero and Henry Arthur Jones, whose dialogue sounds highflown and stagey to our ears. With Archer there's a danger of not being able to see the forest of virtues for the trees of antiquated verbiage.

I would like to go over a few specific things you should notice as you read these plays.

The tragedy of *Rosmersholm* takes place in a gloomy country manor in the windswept north, a house dominated and shadowed by the past. Living there, as the play begins, are the widowed Johannes Rosmer, hereditary master of Rosmersholm, and Rebekka West, the young woman who was his wife's companion and who stayed on after Beata Rosmer died. The country is in political ferment, and the tides of liberalism are rising round those islands of tradition and reaction represented by Rosmersholm and its past. Symbol of this conservatism is Kroll, brother of the dead wife, who tries to enlist Johannes Rosmer in the fight against the new radicalism. But Rosmer is under the spell of the strong-willed, idealistic Rebekka. When he declares for the liberal cause, he makes an implacable enemy of his brother-in-law, Kroll.

Thus, at the outset, in the very first act, the *conflict in the present* is cleanly etched. It will occupy us for most of the remainder of the play. But what has happened in the past, as it is revealed little by little, increasingly intrigues us. We know shortly after the rise of the curtain that the wife, Beata, is dead. But it is some time before we realize that she committed suicide. Later still, we learn that she was demented during the last months of her life, and—apparently without justification—felt that she had to die so that Rosmer could find happiness with

Rebekka. And not until the last great crisis before the play's climax are we given the revelation that makes all clear: Rebekka confesses that she was indeed infatuated with Rosmer. She drove Beata to her death by playing on the crazed wife's fears and suspicions. At this point the past sweeps up and over and completely engulfs the present. Rebekka's confession, which not only exposes her but reveals the tormented Rosmer to himself, is the ultimate step in the long preparation that enables us to accept *Rosmersholm's* fearful ending when Rosmer and Rebekka follow the dead wife (whose presence has been all but tangible throughout) to self-destruction. On all counts, this is a remarkable play, and nowhere more than in the area of exposition and preparation. The story of what has gone before is deliberately doled out to us. We learn about it little by little, and with growing eagerness, as we learned of Blanche's history in *A Streetcar Named Desire.*

Whether *Rosmersholm* is Ibsen's finest play is debatable, but it should be familiar to every writer of drama who respects and loves his craft. Read it for the qualities we have been studying in this and the preceding chapter.

Read *A Doll's House* for the same reason. This play lacks the brooding atmosphere of *Rosmersholm.* It is not as wild and romantic. It is a strong domestic drama of conflict in a middleclass household, and when it was first produced, its characters were recognized as symbols of masculine supremacy and feminine subservience. If we are no longer too interested in Nora Helmer as a symbol of woman struggling to be emancipated, we are captivated by her as a human of complexity and depth. Nora is by turns submissive, playful, enticing, anguished, suicidal, self-willed, and finally supremely strong. But she is fundamentally consistent. You can find a score of instances before the final scene where Nora's behavior is preparing us for her revolutionary break with the past. Nora fascinates actresses as well as audiences: her role is catnip for ambitious stars.

The opening of *A Doll's House* is a deft example of how to start things rolling when the content is nothing more exciting than a family getting ready for Christmas. The scene, between Nora and her husband, Torvald, smuggles in essential exposition: Torvald has just been promoted to the presidency of his bank; they have been somewhat pressed for money, now they will have plenty, but Nora must nevertheless curb her extravagance. Mundane as the chatter is, we are quickly engrossed by their characters, revealed through the talk of promotion and finances. The relationship between the compliant wife—the doll-woman—and the authoritative husband is indelibly drawn. Stern and complacent, Torvald is also fatuous and indulgent. He calls his wife, "my sweet little skylark," "little spendthrift," "Miss Sweettooth," and "my little squirrel." These saccharine endearments underline Torvald's view of his life companion as an irresponsible and presumably backward child who must be alternately coaxed and scolded. Nora's character, in this early stage, is painted more subtly. Superficially, she is what Torvald believes her to be, his pouting, flattering, flirting little woman. But there are hints of the hidden depths that are going to stun Torvald when he eventually discovers them. We become aware, in a piece of trivial business about some macaroons, that Nora is perfectly capable of lying to her husband. When this short scene ends with the entrance of Mrs. Linde, an old friend of Nora, we know much about our two leading characters, and we sense that there will be conflict between them.

Before I leave you to explore the interlocking patterns of *A Doll's House* for yourselves, let me point out one instance that shows the pains Ibsen took with his preparation.

As usual, he has a mountain of information to impart. There is one event we must know right away, before we can get on with the story. Several years before, Torvald was desperately ill, and only a sojourn in a mild climate could save his life. There was no money for such a trip. Furthermore, the doctor felt that the gravity of his condition must be kept from Torvald at any cost. This was the problem Nora solved—by secretly borrowing money, by persuading Torvald that it came from her father, by wheedling him into taking her to sunny Italy. Torvald recovered, and ever since Nora has been paying back the crushing debt with money saved here and pinched there (so much for her alleged extravagance).

We mentioned the entrance of Mrs. Linde, immediately after the first scene. Mrs. Linde is an old and intimate friend whom Nora hasn't seen for nine years.

It would be natural enough if the two old friends, bringing each other up to date, were to discuss the details of Nora's debt. Mrs. Linde has obviously been brought in to be told what the audience must hear.

Pinero and Jones and lesser playwrights would have let it go at that.

But the unadorned device isn't good enough for Ibsen. He adds a touch which makes the situation more natural and also provides a major development in the exposure of Nora's true character. He relates exposition to *growth in the present.*

Mrs. Linde is telling Nora of the problems and hardships she has had to face. At this point we are not sure how much Nora resents her husband's assessment of her as a little birdbrain, but in a moment we will find out. Mrs. Linde patronizingly observes that her sheltered friend knows little of the burdens and troubles of life. When Nora protests, Mrs. Linde smiles and says, "My dear! Small household cares and that sort of thing! You are a child, Nora."

This does it. This echo of her husband's words. Nora flares up: "Don't be so superior . . . You're like all the rest. Thinking I'm incapable of anything really serious . . . that I've gone through nothing in this world of cares. Well—I haven't told you the important thing."

And we are forthwith launched into the exposition. At the same time character is building, since Nora's rebelliousness is more pronounced here than in the opening scene.

I seem to have been deifying Ibsen. But even Homer nodded, and there is one Ibsen play, a very famous one, which I suggest you do not accept as a model of construction. Beware of *Ghosts.*

Ghosts was the great theatrical shocker of its time. The straitlaced audiences of eighty years ago were scandalized by a play which showed the pitiful disintegration of a young artist, victim of the hereditary effect of syphilis contracted by his father. They were further outraged by mention in the second act of the possible advantages of an incestuous union. When the screaming (which lasted two decades) finally died down, *Ghosts* was less emotionally examined and found to be a work of genius. But in preparation and exposition, *Ghosts* has flaws. The back-story comes at us in great blocks. We miss the marvelous deftness of *A Doll's House* and *Rosmersholm.* We are overwhelmed by the narrated past, as we hear of young Oswald's life among the artists in Paris; and the story of Regina, Mrs. Alving's maid, who is really Oswald's half sister; and the biography of Oswald's father, the deceased Captain Alving, responsible for all the trouble, who has a reputation for charity and good works (his wife's doing, actually) but in reality devoted himself to alcoholic and sexual exploits. H. L. Mencken, a pioneer in popularizing Ibsen, surprisingly contended that *Ghosts* did not have a plot. This is a strange assessment. It certainly has enough narrative for two plays and a novel. I think that if you were to summarize the happenings in *Ghosts* briefly, your synopsis would read like the digest of a novel six hundred pages long.

There is an important piece of preparation, too, which shows the kind of thing you should avoid. Mrs. Alving has built an orphanage (a memorial to her late husband!) which she will operate for the community's benefit. She and her confidant, Pastor Manders (she used to be in love with him, if you want more back-story), decide they will not insure the orphanage against fire, because taking out insurance might be interpreted as a lack of trust in divine providence. This is an arbitrary development, to say the least, since it is established that Mrs. Alving has insured every other blessed thing she owns. The conversation occurs in Act One and supplies the first mention of fire. It is an unabashed plant, and it is impossible to miss it. It is followed—not at a decent interval, but almost immediately—by the second mention: Mrs. Alving recalls that there was a small fire in the carpenter's shop at the orphanage, "nothing of any consequence," only the day before. This is the full extent of the preparation for the second act curtain when the Alving drawing room is suffused with a sinister red glow, and Regina screams "Fire!" as the orphanage goes up in flames.

One thing is sure: this clumsy preparation was devised in terms of plot (and symbolism) instead of character. A startling exterior event (the fire) is foreshadowed by exterior preparation (the unlikely decision not to insure against fire).

In its architecture, *Ghosts* resembles those novels of Theodore Dreiser, whose impact, created by sheer, plodding power, staggers us despite faults of construction. Their content makes them great. So it is with *Ghosts*.

Cautionary Conclusions

As I said before, don't burden your own television stories with too much preparation. Choose subjects that do not require overly complicated exposition. Any story you tell is bound to have some of these two elements. Otherwise it wouldn't go anywhere. But steer clear of the plot with a pre-fade in history that, like *Rosmersholm,* is a story in itself. Avoid the character whose motives are so murky, his psyche so warped, and his behavior so contradictory, that you find yourself thrashing around in a labyrinth of invention to make him understandable. Neither you nor television (at present) is equipped to cope with such ambitious conceptions. You lack the experience. Television lacks the time. The hour-length teleplay must, above all, be clear. Half the length: twice as clear.

A few things to remember:

Be sure a character behaves from the beginning in a manner consistent with the way he will react to a crisis.

As you invent incident to depict his character, be sure the incident is (1) entertaining, (2) not dragged in by the hair of its head to make your point—in other words, not revealed under improbable circumstances or at an unlikely time, and (3) not emphasized so heavily that it causes your audience to anticipate a happening you do not want to reveal prematurely.

Present your exposition, in most cases, little by little. Do not stop the flow of your teleplay to divulge information. Your characters must be involved in the present as they impart the past. See to it that the spectator is interested in both.

It is a danger signal when you sense that you are putting in exposition not really too interesting just to make your teleplay work. We all come to such obstacles in drama writing: you need a certain scene but, as you write it, you are suddenly not as absorbed in it as you were in other scenes. Something is wrong. Now is the time to back away and take a long, calm, objective look at your material.

You may realize the scene is *not* essential, that dropping it out improves your story.

Or it may dawn on you that you are not giving certain vital lines to the right character. The moribund scene springs to life when another person takes over the exposition.

Another possibility: you may be introducing the expository scene too early. If it comes later on, when your story has gained momentum, it automatically acquires the interest you felt was missing.

But—suppose you have tried all these remedies and nothing works. Major surgery is required, because you see that the trouble is not in the scene itself, it lies elsewhere. (George S. Kaufman, once in great demand as a play doctor, said, "When I'm told they're having second act trouble, I immediately look at the first act to see what's wrong.") Any writer is dismayed to discover that his basic concept is faulty. But it happens. It's a trouble of the trade. You will have to rethink your story, determine what is wrong where, and then do the necessary work of revision, even if it means starting all over with a radical new approach to your material.

Be honest, admit the fundamental fault; don't fool yourself and try to fix things by changing that one scene if what is demanded is a major rewrite. Television producers and story editors are notorious for detecting patch-up jobs. They also have an irritating habit of spouting clichés such as "Good shows aren't written, they're rewritten."

IV

The Motion Picture Form

Television's history is troubled. Uncertainty has been present at every stage of its progress. The medium is more chaotic at present than the movies were at the same age. Television (I am talking about the commercial, sponsored variety) is prone to change without notice and without reason.

Let two or three dramatic programs fail to rack up satisfactory ratings during this season, and next season will see a mad scramble to put "situation comedy" on the home screen. When a few of these comedies fail (due to pressure, lack of preparation time, and pervading boneheadedness), the impresarios will jettison the laugh tracks and go after something different. Somebody will rediscover the Western. Somebody else will devise a show that can be photographed under water. What our producers will not do is ask themselves if a program failed because the television audience did not really want that kind of program, or whether it failed because it was lousy. (This demented approach to What the Public Wants, it is only fair to remember, did not originate in television. With its attendant confusion, it has always been characteristic of show business. It was never more pronounced than in the case of television's immediate ancestor, the motion picture, whose producers also knew there was no such thing as a bad show, only good pictures that capricious audiences didn't patronize because they wanted comedy instead of heart-warming drama, or musicals instead of westerns, or gangster melodramas instead of historical spectacles.)

The prospect before us is hazy, but one pattern seems to take shape out of the blur: theater movies and television pictures are becoming more alike. In a physical sense this movement of television in the direction of the movies is obvious. The confined, studio-produced television dramas that were broadcast "live" a few years ago are almost entirely superseded by filmed screenplays photographed by the same cameras used for shooting movies designed to be shown in theaters instead of being broadcast over the channels of the television networks. There are hopeful indications also that the producers responsible for the content of dramatic television are beginning to reach for the maturity of theatrical features. The progress, it must be admitted, is of a glacial slowness and is consistently impeded by the success of those inane programs which continue to find favor with the less discriminating sections of the television audience. Nevertheless, a new thoughtfulness and a new frankness, a more pronounced depth in approach, and a willingness to deal with less juvenile story subject matter are detectable in some areas. Here and there, too, the stories for television films tend to be longer (despite the popularity of the half-hour telefilm which doubtless, considering the nature of home viewing, will always be with us) in the length style of conventional theater movies. Two hour features, as well as those at the ninety minute Movie of the Week length, today occupy much of television's prime time. Even longer pictures are serialized. If the writer is to take full advantage of his television market, he will absorb much that is helpful from watching theater movies.

So far, we have concentrated on principles that hold good for every dramatic form. It is time for a good look at those which relate solely to the film medium. Remember: they apply to stories written for the television tube as well as those intended for the theater screen.

Viewing and Hearing

In Jean Anouilh's *Becket,* as it was written for the stage, a development at the end of the first act afforded us an unnerving example of Thomas Becket's devotion to Henry, his comrade and his king. Becket has persuaded the lecherous monarch to refrain from deflowering a Saxon peasant girl, but King Henry demands "favor for favor," and Becket gives his word to grant the King's wish. To his dismay, Becket is asked to turn over his beloved mistress Gwendolen for Henry's enjoyment. Bitterly honoring his pledge, Becket sends the girl to the King. A while later, Henry stumbles into Becket's chambers, shaken and aghast. He says, "I had no pleasure with her, Thomas. She let me lay her down in the litter, limp as a corpse, and then suddenly she pulled out a little knife from somewhere. There was blood everywhere . . . I feel quite sick." He adds, "She could easily have killed me instead!"

When *Becket* was made into a motion picture, this sequence was treated somewhat differently. Becket sent his mistress off to the King, as in the play version. But at this point, a new scene was written: we saw Henry approach the curtained litter or palanquin where the girl awaited him. We saw him pull back the curtain and then freeze in his tracks. We cut to the interior of the litter and, in a shocking close shot, saw Gwendolen lying dead, a dagger hilt protruding from her body. There was no need for "blood everywhere." The ghastly pallor, the limp figure told us Gwendolen was dead. There was a close-up of Henry's horrified face, and then he staggered off to tell Becket the news. The rest of the sequence was like the play version.

The two ways of treating the same episode—*telling* it on the stage, *showing* it on the screen—demonstrate how a proper use of movie technique can strengthen dramatic incident. No matter how vividly Henry describes what he has just seen—the very act of suicide—his words can never shake us as does our brief glimpse of the dead girl lying in the litter. And even if it were practical to add an extra scene on the stage and show us Henry discovering the body, the result would inevitably be feebler, because we could not see the essential detail of tragedy that the close shot—the camera within a few inches of its subject—provides. In choosing to make this departure from the original, trifling as it may be in the over-all effect, Edward Anhalt, who adapted Anouilh's play to the screen, realized the full value of his medium.

We all accept the fact that movies can do things not possible on the stage. The screen depicts spectacular reality, it fabricates fantasy, it summons history to our view. As a medium that permits action on a very large scale, it offers the writer great freedom. This opportunity for bigness, subject only to economic discipline, is obvious and need not be labored.

It is more important for the writer to understand that the film form is capable of more subtlety—small-scale action, if you like—than the drama has ever known before. The camera, and therefore the audience, can be so close to a character that his every reaction registers. A point is made without a word being said, whereas in the theater spoken comment is necessary if the spectator in the last row is to follow what's going on. In writing a scene, think carefully before putting down such dialogue as "I see what you mean," "I can't believe it," "That's the most shocking thing I ever heard," and similar lines that express only a character's state of mind or emotion, his *reaction* to something said or done. Since your aim is to be as natural and lifelike as possible, you will often conclude that a lifted eyebrow, a perplexed frown, or an ironic smile will put over what you want to convey more effectively than a "stagey" exclamation. Just be certain that you clearly describe the expression on your character's face and that you are in a close shot at the time. The camera will do the rest.

Mobility

The camera can get close to its subject.

The other important thing to remember is that the camera can move.

It follows people, it rolls back as a character walks towards it, it moves towards an object we wish to see in detail, it accompanies a running figure, it traverses an interesting setting, moving from left to right or vice-versa, showing the audience minute objects of the locale.

Conveniently, we shall assume two kinds of camera movement: automatic mobility and mobility for a purpose. The automatic kind is a function of the director and the cameraman, and it is not necessary for the writer to indicate it in his script. To avoid confusion, let's see exactly what it is. Suppose you have written a brief scene in which physical action is unimportant. Two girls and a man are having a conversation in an office. The talk is the main thing. It's a dialogue scene, a static scene. But when the director stages it, to keep things easy and natural, to prevent it from being *too* static, he introduces certain negligible but realistic pieces of business. The man goes to a desk to get a cigarette while he talks, one of the girls nervously sits down and gets up again, the other moves back when the man gets too close to her. Part of the time we will be in a medium shot, with all three people visible, and, as they move about, the camera will move with them, sometimes only slightly, to keep them within the shot. This is automatic camera movement, and it lends fluidity to the scene. Turn on television, look at almost any program, and you are bound to see this slight but constant camera movement. It has become so commonplace that you probably wouldn't notice it if you weren't looking for it. Dismiss it from your mind. You don't have to bother with it in your script.

Frequently, however, you will find reason to use the moving camera; a scene in your story demands it, or will benefit by it. This is the second kind: camera movement for a purpose. There are a number of ways of indicating this movement in your script, depending on what you want to show. You can say CAMERA PANS or CAMERA MOVES. The term PAN SHOT (pan is short for panorama) is generally used when you want the camera to move across a set, or across a group of characters. This moving shot is also known as a DOLLY SHOT, a "dolly" being the platform on wheels which supports the camera. Harking back to Chapter I, remember that any movement of the camera should be in capitals in the body of your direction. Three examples:

```
John rises from his chair and crosses to the door at the end
of the room, CAMERA PANNING with him.

Murray, instead of answering her question, turns on his heel
and strides away. CAMERA FOLLOWS him.

CAMERA PANS across the crowded aisle of the temple, from
LEFT TO RIGHT, past the money-changers' booths, the sellers
of doves, and the groups of people clustered around them.
```

The terminology of camera movement is not supremely important (after all, the word MOVES will cover almost anything you want to do). What *is* vital is the necessity for you to visualize a scene's action in every detail. See before you write. Picture the movement in your mind, and then describe it. Your mental vision must be on the job from FADE IN on the first page to FADE OUT on the last. In fiction, presenting a vivid scene by cataloguing incidents is not always desirable. You may want the reader to rely on his imagination to conjure up essential elements. You mention one or two suggestive objects or motions to evoke setting and atmosphere, because your concern, say, is the dialogue. But writing playscript or teleplay or screenplay is a most literal business; your words have to be translated into images, and nothing of consequence that takes place in the physical action can be omitted from your directions. We are not, remember, talking about those bits of naturalistic motion the director puts in.

Some gifted and intelligent people lack this ability to visualize. To them, reading a play or a movie script gives no pleasure; it is a chore, because they cannot see in the mind's eye the scene and the action as it is laid out for them on the printed page. To visualize, to absorb in terms of pictures, is an instant and instinctive process. A writer who lacks it is better employed in another literary field, for the purpose of writing drama is to create something that will be seen.

A handy, labor-saving direction is CAMERA FOLLOWS ACTION. It is correctly used for a scene of complicated action, which will be photographed with considerable camera movement and probably in several cuts (or shots). The experienced writer knows that he cannot predict what the director and cameraman will want to do when they come to lay out the mechanical steps of shooting his scene. So, instead of trying to outguess them and indicate the camera's various moves, he describes the *action itself* in one master scene, and writes at the conclusion, CAMERA FOLLOWS ACTION.

How to Write It

I'll show you an example. Let's go back to the two girls and the man in the office, and call them John, Jill, and Mary. John is determined to post a certain letter (for reasons which I do not propose to go into) and Jill and Mary are equally resolved to get hold of the letter and destroy it. At a certain point, the dialogue scene explodes into action. Grasping the letter, John starts for the door and breaks into a run as the girls try to intercept him. He rushes through the office door leading to the corridor outside, with Jill and Mary in close pursuit, and we cut to

```
INT. CORRIDOR     MEDIUM SHOT     DAY

John comes rushing out of the office and races towards the
mail chute at the end of the corridor, near the elevators.
Jill and Mary are at his heels. As Mary overtakes him, she
makes a wild grab for the letter clutched in John's right
```

```
hand. He eludes her, only to be brought up short as Jill
tackles him around the waist. He staggers, loses his bal-
ance, and goes sprawling. The letter slips out of his hand.
Mary picks it up and sprints back towards the office, as
John and Jill scramble to their feet. CAMERA FOLLOWS ACTION.
```

We are so accustomed to camera mobility in the movies that it is a shock to realize films were in existence as popular entertainment for a quarter of a century before the camera began to move and explore its subjects. During most of the silent picture era, one scene followed another as the story unfolded, from long shot to close to medium, and the actors moved around but the camera didn't. In 1914 D. W. Griffith put his camera on the back of a truck for a battle scene in *The Birth of a Nation,* and we saw the Little Colonel leading a Confederate charge right into the camera which kept ahead of the onrush for a shot of considerable duration. A few other abortive usages of the moving camera can be found in primitive motion pictures; they are abortive because their value as examples of technique was not grasped and they remained unimitated except by accident. In 1903 Edwin S. Porter, generally credited with making the first movie to tell a story, *The Great Train Robbery,* panned his camera twice in that film to cover action scenes involving his outlaw characters. But it was not until the early 1920's, the last decade of silent cinema, that the Germans put the camera on wheels, or on the end of a crane, and gave movies a startling new flow. The German technique, revealed in such pictures as *The Last Laugh* and *Variety,* involved not only a mobile camera but experimental lighting and radical camera angles. It was quickly adapted by studios the world over and became a part of film grammar.

Long before the great technical improvements that began in the third decade of this century, the movies learned a potent lesson: don't imitate the stage. Show it instead of talking about it. We have seen how valid that principle is today in the example from *Becket.*

The lesson was not learned quickly or easily. Sixty years ago, in their infancy, the movies were a sorrowful imitation of the stage (*The Great Train Robbery* to the contrary notwithstanding). Many of them seemed hardly more than photographed records of theatrical performances. Sarah Bernhardt appeared before the camera in her role of Queen Elizabeth (prints of the picture are still in existence) and, after expiring in the final scene, rose up and took a bow to climax a dull and static picture.

Motion, pantomime, some notion of the medium's possibilities, arrived with slapstick comedy and two-reel Westerns. These pictures were rich in violent action. They abounded in situations which the stage could never encompass. Sight gags and frantic shadow play liberated the film, and out of these early essays in *movement* grew the great mimed technique of the movies that flowered in the middle 1920's. When pictures started to talk, they briefly lost their mobility. Primitive sound recording that imposed severe restrictions on the camera took them back a score of years to the period of photographed stage plays. For a year or two, audiences were fed a diet of stodgy if raucous cinema. Only the novelty of sound made these crude pieces acceptable. Fortunately, the microphone's mysteries were rapidly mastered, and the ironic retrogression was succeeded by a satisfactory blending of the visual and the aural. The technique was years old and solidly established when television took it over.

The Differences

There are some differences between theater movies and televised films, and we certainly shall not ignore them, even though they are in the realm of the obvious. If *Becket* had been made into a telefilm, instead of a lavish theatrical feature, economic factors would have dictated a more modest production, and a quantity of pageantry and spectacle would have been sacrificed. But the visual treatment of Gwendolen's death would have had the same heightened impact on the smaller television screen. The image of the girl in the litter, the close-up of Henry's face—these are pure cinema however you project them.

What you *cannot* do on television that you *can* do in a theatrical movie is largely a matter of judgment and common sense. Huge mob scenes and towering sets are far less impressive in the former medium, even if the television budget could afford them. Don't write the Fall of Babylon into your script.

Also, you shouldn't need to be reminded that censorship standards in television, because of the limitless family audience, are considerably more stringent than those obtaining elsewhere. We have all heard lines in contemporary theatrical films which if spoken on a popular television show through some monstrous accident would doubtless shake the social structure. But there is considerably more freedom on the air today than in 1966, when the first edition of this book was published. Then, an occasional "hell" and "damn" in the dialogue and a gingerly approach to such story subjects as prostitution and homosexuality were about as far as the networks would permit you to go. In 1974 the social scene is being far more honestly reflected. One of many influences responsible for the new maturity is undoubtedly the series of multiepisode telefilms produced in England and rebroadcast here—*Pére Goriot* and *Cousin Bette,* for example, with their unrepressed examination of a dissolute society.

Here again your best guides are judgment and common sense. Add good taste. And a useful rule of thumb is writing for television what you would write for a motion picture that bears the rating G (for general audiences) or at most PG (parental guidance advised). You don't have to confine yourself to Peter Rabbit, of course, but Fritz the Cat still isn't tame enough for the tube.

V

An Exercise in Adaptation

The methods you will use in writing your story for a visual medium can be fixed firmly in your mind if you will now explore some of the problems that arise in adapting a piece of fiction or, as we shall consider specifically, a stage play to the theater or television screen. There is also an excellent long-range reason for you to understand the procedure: if you become a successful writer for movies or television, you will almost certainly be given assignments to write screenplays or teleplays based on stories or stage plays which are the work of somebody else. No matter how faithful you determine to make your script to the original, you will find yourself changing a great many things about the plot incident and the characters so that they will be displayed to maximum advantage in their new visual form.

The tasks in adapting a novel or a play to the screen are to some degree the same as those you will meet in writing an original teleplay. Before you start the teleplay itself, you should have your plot points and character descriptions down on paper in some kind of sequence so that you know exactly where you are going. When this has been done to your satisfaction, you will proceed to *adapt* your own outline into its final, visual, scene-by-scene format. For these reasons I would like to go over with you the methods of adaptation by applying them to a specific subject. You are familiar with *Rosmersholm*, so let's use that for our example. (I am not suggesting that you undertake the staggering task of turning Ibsen's drama into a teleplay; only that you examine it as though you were going to do so.)

Rosmersholm makes a challenging exercise. It calls for ingenuity and imagination. It is a completely static play, its physical action confined to entrances and exits and short walks between furniture. But its story, as we have seen, refers to a lot of dramatic incident that happened before the opening, and also action that takes place off stage in the present is described in the dialogue. There are obvious visual opportunities here.

Assume that a producer has assigned you to adapt *Rosmersholm* into a two-hour teleplay. He wants it reasonably faithful to Ibsen, but he does *not* want just a film record of a stage play. So you have freedom to put some movement into the piece.

Cutting and Condensing

A certain amount of cutting is necessary to put this long play into two hours. It should not be radical. You will find it much easier to trim dialogue throughout the play than to shorten it by dropping an entire scene.

Pick a scene which seems to you relatively placid and pare it down to its essentials. You will find places where you can eliminate lines and even whole speeches in the first and second acts. The second half of the play, with its steadily rising intensity and its tightly knit narrative, is not so easy to cut.

One sequence that can be edited occurs in the first act when Rosmer's brother-in-law, Kroll, discourses at length about his insubordinate family. This dialogue can be drastically condensed, thereby sharpening the scene's principal point: to establish that Rosmer's liberal views are in conflict with Kroll's conservatism. Go over the four acts and see what other parts you can find to shorten. Be judicious: don't blue-pencil anything vital to the story line. On the other hand, don't be too reverent. After all, producers cut *Hamlet,* sometimes dropping out major characters (Fortinbras, Rosenkranz, and Guildenstern) altogether.

All right. Consider the editing done. *Rosmersholm* is down to size. You are ready to introduce some cinematic changes . . . to retell (without violating) Ibsen's drama so that it reaches your audience as a televised film and not just as a photographed stage play.

First and simplest of the methods you can use is to shift the setting of an actionless sequence to give it the illusion of motion. Instead of having Rosmer and Rebekka West play a scene in the drawing room, take them out into the garden, and have them walk up and down as they talk. Write in natural movement—a sudden stop, a turning away—to underscore salient dialogue. Ibsen's play is confined to the drawing room and to Rosmer's study: your setting is the whole somber mansion and the northern countryside that surrounds it.

An important secondary character is the housekeeper, Mrs. Helseth, with what Eva Le Gallienne calls "her crude peasant awareness of occult forces." There are several good scenes between her and Rebekka: move one of them out of the drawing room and let it take place in the kitchen, as Mrs. Helseth prepares dinner. Shift another to a bedroom and show the two women counting linen while they play their scene. This physical trivia of everyday life, consistently inserted throughout the script, will give the film version at least a portion of the visual flow it wants. In the film of *The Best Man,* Vidal switched locales all the time. A first-act scene, static in a hotel room on the stage, was changed to the grounds of the Ambassador in Los Angeles, with political figures racing around and a helicopter landing and taking off. The content was the same, but the story broke away from the shackles of the stage and became sheer movie.

Opening Things Up

Now we come to the major part of this exercise. We must determine what parts of this play can be shown instead of talked about. Their selection is a very delicate matter. It is not a case of indiscriminately translating sound into sight, dialogue into action. Some of the things talked about are not essentially pictorial. Others, referred to with fear and trembling by the characters in this highly romantic tragedy, would lose their force if they were fully revealed. Finally, there are dialogue scenes of great power and conflict which *must* play as Ibsen wrote them. They may seem to offer opportunities for flashbacks, for visualizing, but any deviation from their continuity will destroy their power. Such a scene is Rebekka's confession, at the end of the third act, that she drove Rosmer's wife to her death.

Deciding what scenes you can open up and pictorialize, and which ones you *cannot* meddle with, is a fascinating operation.

Don't carry it out in a vacuum.

Do it with a fellow student. Discuss, argue, contradict, hold firm, and give in. You would frequently communicate with both your producer and director in just this way if your adaptation were the real thing instead of a dry run.

Such an exchange—resulting in the discovery that some of your ideas are faulty; the conviction that others, although opposed, are sound—gives you the stimulus of excitement and enthusiasm to do a good job.

The first opportunity to make a constructive cinematic change comes with the curtain's rise on Act One of *Rosmersholm.* (The quotation that follows is from Ann Jellicoe's translation.) [1] The scene, as Ibsen wrote it, is the drawing room on a summer evening, and Rebekka West sits sewing by the window. Mrs. Helseth, the housekeeper, comes in, and comments that Rebekka is sitting in a draft. She starts to close the window. Looking out, she says, "Isn't that the Pastor there now?" Rebekka's startled reaction strikes us as a bit extreme. She rises hastily and joins Mrs. Helseth at the window. Stationing herself behind the curtain, she says, "Keep back. Don't let him see us."

MRS. HELSETH [*moving back into the room*] What do you know, he's started to use the mill path again.

REBECCA He took the mill path the day before yesterday as well. [*peeping out between the curtains and the window frame*] But now we shall see—

MRS. HELSETH Is he going over the footbridge?

REBECCA That's what I want to see. [*after a moment*] No, he's turned off. Going by the upper road today as well, [*leaves window*] the long way round.

MRS. HELSETH Oh dear me yes. It must be hard for the Pastor to cross the footbridge where a thing like that's happened, and—

REBECCA [*putting her crochet together*] They cling to their dead here at Rosmersholm.

Ibsen is well on his way. Within sixty seconds of his opening, he has shown us one of his two leading characters, talked about the other in a most intriguing manner, and hinted at the play's subject and theme. We know that a man named Rosmer dreads crossing a certain bridge

[1] Henrik Ibsen, *Rosmersholm,* translated by Ann Jellicoe. Copyright © 1961 by Chandler Publishing Company.

because of an event that took place there. And we know that the event was almost certainly a death.

Well and good for the stage. But you have the means, withheld from Ibsen, of doing more with this opening. You can make it more impressive. And you will do no violence to the original.

Remember that an important element of *Rosmersholm* is atmosphere. The spirit of the ancient dwelling, where painted ancestors look sternly down from the walls, "where children have never been known to cry . . . and when they grow up . . . never laugh," hangs fog-like over the play. It is a weird house where fears from the past obsess the living.

Let us include this quality in our beginning.

FADE IN on the first of several shots depicting this dominating place. It is a summer evening. Let your camera portray the contrast between the tranquility of trees and garden, and the forbidding, sinister, craggy outlines of the house. Then, in a long shot, pick up Rosmer's lonely figure walking along the path that leads to the bridge over the foaming mill stream. Hold on him until he gets close to the bridge and slows his pace. Go to a medium close shot as he comes to a halt and stares at the rushing water. A close-up reveals the mingled indecision and anguish on his face. Now, cut back to Rosmersholm, and let us see the window where Rebekka and the housekeeper are watching intently and with concern. Next, a medium shot of the distressed Rosmer. The camera can follow him as he backs away from the bridge, turns, and almost rushes towards the upper road. As he moves off, we cut to the interior of the drawing room at the moment the two women turn away from the window. The first words (of the picture version) are spoken. Mrs. Helseth looks at the silent Rebekka and exclaims: "Good Lord! You can't blame him for not wanting to cross that bridge, Miss. . . ." And so on, as we pick up the dialogue from the play, and continue into the next scene.

We have gotten rid of the device, indigenous to the stage, of having Mrs. Helseth notice that Rebekka is in a draught, thus giving her reason to go to the window, look out, see Rosmer, and summon Rebekka. We are, too, relieved of the necessity of having the women tell each other and the audience what they see. We have substituted pure motion picture technique, expositorily efficient, dramatically as effective, and possessed of the added value of showing us what Rosmer looks like, and the appearance of the house itself.

See if you can find another place where this cinematic treatment will better the story.

Dramatizing the Intangible

Before we conclude this exercise, it is important to call your attention to two elements that pervade the play and that you will have to deal with. They are symbolistic in nature, rather strange, and each suggests a number of film treatments. I shall leave to you the question of which approach to use.

The first is the presence of the dead wife, Beata. She is talked about, and what she did profoundly affects the destinies of Rosmer and Rebekka. She is more than a ghost. She is a motivational force, an unseen member of the cast. A major accomplishment of the play is to keep us continually conscious of a person who isn't there. Shall we simply preserve this eerie quality by leaving it unchanged? Alfred Hitchcock, when he filmed Daphne DuMaurier's novel, *Rebecca,* was faced with a similar problem. He solved it by adhering to the book. He never introduced the title character, the dead wife around whom the story revolved.

But you may decide to employ the resources of the screen, regardless of Ibsen's intent. Since Beata motivates what happens in *Rosmersholm,* let us show what she does, see what happens to her. Instead of hearing about her fate from her brother, and from the sly editor, Mortensgaard, we can witness the events that marked her path to madness and destruction.

Now there is a third way to handle the story of Beata. It is a way of compromise, and it is a device peculiar to the movie screen. You couldn't use it in any other medium. It is eating your cake and having it too. (Please bear in mind I am not recommending any of these approaches. I am pointing them out. The choice is yours.)

Suppose that when Kroll reveals to Rosmer the visit paid him by Rosmer's wife—a visit establishing the fact that Beata knew what was happening to her and to her husband—we use the familiar device of the dissolve, and go into a flashback. We are on a close shot of Kroll. We see him at the door of his house, admitting Beata. We see his reactions as we hear what she says. Possibly, in another shot, we see the back of her head. But never, in this visualized retrospect, do we see her face. This is what I mean by eating your cake and having it, too. It is possible to go into the past and and show what the play could only talk about. But we do it in such a way that we preserve the play's device of never allowing the audience to see this important character.

The other matter we must determine involves the White Horse. *Rosmersholm* is filled with symbols, but Ibsen insists on none as strongly as this image that stands for Death. We hear about it in the play's very first scene between Rebekka and Mrs. Helseth, and it is referred to a dozen times during the course of the play. The White Horse, a ghostly presence, is naturally never seen; but Mrs. Helseth gives it first place in her private mythology. And Rebekka, skeptical as she is, is fascinated by the symbol.

The White Horse is surely too good a thing to pass up. What shall we do with him?

Keep cutting away to the mystical stallion every time he is mentioned in the dialogue?

Use him more sparingly, perhaps showing him behind the credit titles at the opening?

Or shall we deliberately withhold his image, perhaps tantalizing our audience, until the play's explosive finish, and then, just before Rebekka and Rosmer cast themselves into the mill stream, cut to an impressionistic shot of the rearing, raging animal?

There may well be other ways to integrate the White Horse. Choose what you will. I suggest only that he should not remain a mere figure of speech.

VI

Writer and Director

At the beginning of this book you read that the writer should always be economical in his use of camera directions.

The first of the two main reasons for this is obvious: a script is much easier to read if every page isn't cluttered with a lot of directions. The first people to read your script—the story editor, the producer, and any other executives sharing the decision to buy or not to buy your teleplay—should not have their attention diverted from its story values by constant reminders that now we're in a close shot and here we go to a medium one. They all know a finished picture will have ten times the shots indicated in your script.

You may wonder why we have spent so much time on the camera directions if you are going to use them with such restraint.

Because it is vital that you get the ones you do use *right*.

When your script is bought for production, it will be read by all sorts of technicians: the cameraman, the costume or wardrobe people, set designers, casting directors, film editors, sound engineers, and the network's director of continuity acceptance (the censor, in plain English). These craftsmen are your fellow workers, and your script is their guide. Give them the benefit of clear, professional directions, directions which will insure that the makers of your picture know *how* you want it made.

The second reason for not overburdening your teleplay with camera shots has to do with the director. He is the most important person to you in the whole complex procedure of turning your story into a motion picture for television; for when the pages of your teleplay pass from your hands to his, the director becomes responsible for the transformation of your material from words into images. Supervising the contributory work of a score of technicians, he plays the major part in changing a tele*play* into a tele*film*. He plans each scene and determines how much coverage (number of shots) to give it, his decision being determined by its importance in the script. The directions you have written down will tell him in general how a scene is to go. It is his job to expand and elaborate—building on the foundation you have given him.

The director's superior (and yours) is the producer, but he is mainly an administrator. The producer buys your story; he decides how much money to spend on shooting it; he can demand certain changes in the story; and, in consultation with the director, he casts the picture. In these preparatory stages the director usually has a good deal of authority, and on the set during the shooting of the picture he is supremely in charge.

Words into Pictures

You should understand exactly what happens to your script when it goes before the camera. Look at that scene in the first chapter, the one with Sylvia and Thorpe. All we have is the beginning, but let's suppose that the scene goes on for four pages, that it's structurally important, that it involves only these two people, and that it is a scene in which the dialogue is the essential thing, with no physical action to speak of. Let's further assume that you have set it down in a medium close shot, three close-ups, and a close two shot. The medium close shot is to show something of the setting, and you have put in the closer angles for dramatic emphasis.

Now, because the scene is so important, the director decides to photograph it in a number of ways, to give it what he calls "full coverage." He deliberately shoots more film than he will use so that when he edits it he will have a lot of footage from which to make his final selection (as commonly expressed: "Enough film so we can play around with the scene").

First, he will shoot a master sequence, probably in a medium shot, in which the actors play the scene from start to finish. Second, he has them go through it again in a close shot. Next, the camera is turned on

Sylvia, and she repeats her performance in a close-up, with Thorpe reading his lines out of camera range. Thorpe then gets his close-up. If this were a feature with a long schedule, instead of a telefilm the director must finish shooting in six days, he would embellish the sequence with shots taken from other angles. He would also try to obtain top quality by shooting the same angle several times, and would then discard all but the one "take" in which he felt the best performance was given. In the opulent, pre-television days of 1944, when shooting schedules were fantastically long, and thoroughness was occasionally confused with waste, a scene in a feature based on Oscar Wilde's *The Picture of Dorian Gray*—a modest passage of talk between two people in a hansom cab—was photographed forty-four times before the perfectionist directing the picture secured the delicate dialogue nuances he was after. Television, as we know, went that-a-way in the opposite, equally deplorable direction of the speed-up; but despite its truncated shooting time, the Thorpe-Sylvia scene will be recorded on at least five times the amount of film that will be seen on the tube.

Cutting (editing) the scene is a process of selection. The director keeps in mind such things as quality of acting (which is bound to vary from shot to shot), pace, rhythm, and dramatic effectiveness as he chooses and puts together segments of the different shots to form the scene as it will be finally seen. He may feel that things should move faster. He can speed up the action because he has several shots of the same happenings to pick from.

When the scene was played on the set, there was a slight pause between something Sylvia said and Thorpe's reply. The pause occurs in every shot because it was the way they played the scene. But on close examination the director feels that this pause makes the scene lag just when it should accelerate. Therefore, the instant the last word is spoken by Sylvia in a two shot, the director cuts to a close-up of Thorpe, and has Thorpe's opening words come so close on the end of Sylvia's speech as to eliminate any hint of hesitation. He can repeat the process at any point where he wishes to speed up the tempo because the amount of film he has taken makes it possible to "play around" with the scene.

Throughout, the director at his discretion has cut from two shot to close-up to medium shot to another close-up, with the result that your four-page scene, which had five shots, emerges on the screen as a series of twenty-two separate shots or cuts.

They were all based on, or at least suggested by, those five camera angles which you correctly inserted. There will be occasions during the writing of a teleplay when you are doubtful as to what kind of camera angle to indicate. These occasions should not be too frequent if you have thoroughly visualized your action. But when you are honestly puzzled about whether a passage of dialogue or a scene of action should be played in a close shot (for instance) or in a medium shot, it is permissible to write ANGLE ON (followed by the names of the characters in the shot) as the heading for the scene and let the director choose the kind of angle he wants. Examples of this approach will be found in James E. Moser's teleplay from the program *Slattery's People,* reproduced in the appendix.

Although it is not the writer's problem, you may be amused to hear that factors other than dramatic considerations enter into the director's selection of his shots when he starts editing. Actors and actresses love close-ups. They know that even a chiseled profile can look blurred in a medium shot when it is projected on that small television screen. It has been known to happen that an actor who reads a speech effectively in a close-up turns unaccountably mush-mouthed when the camera is moved away more than four feet from his features. Faced with a bad reading in a medium shot or a fine one in a close-up, the director makes the obvious choice.

Staying with It

When the director starts to function, the writer's role is diminished: he is no longer in charge of his story. Should the writer feel resentful when this happens? No. But he generally does. Many writers have become directors, so strong is the urge to exert control over one more stage of their work. Many others would like to.

A more present help for that feeling of frustration is the honest admission that nowhere in the region of creative writing is the writer so dependent on other people as he is in that latter stage when his teleplay (or motion picture script) is being translated into a film. He needs cooperation and he must give cooperation. When principal photography (the term for the actual shooting of a movie) begins, he must rely on the efforts of all sorts of workers, besides the director, if his creation is to see the light and itself be seen in a favorable light. Very few film artists (and no television artists that I know of) attain such eminence that they can control what happens to their material from the cradle to the box office. Francois Truffaut in France (*Jules and Jim, The Four Hundred Blows, Soft Skin*) collaborates on the writing of his screenplays, directs them, and shares responsibility with his producer. William Wyler, as both producer and director, closely oversees the writing of his pictures. The unique instance of the movie creator responsible only to himself is Charlie Chaplin. He wrote his scripts, performed them, directed them, composed their music, and supervised them down to such a detail as selecting the size of the screen they would be projected on at their first runs.

That the writer today is not altogether excluded from the production of his scripts, that he *can* in most cases stay with the picture through its later phases, can be credited to the Writers Guild of America (formerly the Screen Writers Guild). In Chapter XI you will learn of the Guild's importance to you. For the moment, note that the Guild has struggled unceasingly not only to get monetary benefits for its members, but to secure for them the recognition, the esteem, the dignity, that simply did not exist a few decades ago.

What happens when the script of your teleplay passes from your hands? How do you behave?

Well—assume this is a few years hence. You are in demand as a writer. Your agent is getting you so many offers of writing assignments that you are obliged to turn down some, and this hurts because you are the dedicated type who wants to make a lot of money. You have performed all the rewriting on the current assignment called for by your contract. Oh, the script might be improved, the director might like some work beyond the call of duty, but legally you are in the clear. So—on to the next assignment. And the next, and the next.

I hope you are beginning to suspect that this is not an altogether wholesome approach to creative film writing. Nor is it, in the long run, a profitable one. The writer who holds this view will probably become a successful hack, and then an unsuccessful one. He will burn out himself and his reputation by too much work performed to nobody's satisfaction.

The writers for television whose work stays in demand have this in common: they want to keep an eye on their pictures until the film is in the can. They make suggestions when suggestions are called for. They are ready to alter the script if unforeseen production problems come up. And, realizing that making a picture is team work, they consider themselves on the team.

On the Set

But your immediate problem is not dealing with the heady temptations of success. It is how to proceed when, as a novice, you have sold your first script and it is approved for production.

I must assume in this discussion of the relationship between the writer and director that the writer lives somewhere near the center of television production. If he does not at the time his first script is sold, he probably will very shortly thereafter.

The writer usually will be welcome on the set during shooting, and even during rehearsals and other preliminaries. Take full advantage of this opportunity, for it is a most important part of your education. When you go on the sound stage for the first time, you will not be a stranger, at least not to the director. By this time you have established some kind of rapport with him, because he has met you during the rewriting, or final editing, of the script. He has made suggestions. So have you. You have discussed character and structure together. You may have argued heatedly. Don't let such conflict disturb you; it is normal in the writer-director relationship. If you have won your point, he will respect you. And if he has convinced *you,* he will love and cherish you.

It is not possible to overestimate the value to the new television writer of sticking close to the physical production of his first screenplays. The amount of information he will absorb, information that will help his future writings, is remarkable. As he watches the preparation and playing of one scene, he will gain insight that hours of concentration on theory will never fix as firmly in his mind.

Haunt the set. Talk to the camera crew, the assistant directors, the players, carpenters, grips (stagehands), and electricians. But above all —watch.

Do you want to direct some day? If so, you should become familiar with everything from reflectors and booms to dialogue rehearsal and set decoration. Be an observer, an eavesdropper, and a conversational gadfly. (Watch the conversation, though. Shooting a picture involves periods of intense concentration as a scene is shot, punctuated by moments of relaxation for everybody but those technicians who are setting up and lighting the next scene for the director's approval. Be sure you ask your questions during these relaxed breaks.)

If you don't want to direct, but intend to stick to your typewriter, then the studio sound stage is still the place for your advanced education. You will behold the practical application of what you have been learning. You will see the director introduce, on the spur of the moment, a bit of business that enhances the humor in a comedy scene. You will suddenly realize that a certain speech you wrote strikes a false note when it is articulated. You will accept the need to rephrase it so it will sound more natural. You will see the director improve an elaborate action scene by simplifying it and speeding it up.

Become a fixture on the set during your early career. Get people used to seeing you around. They will accept you and soon come to regard you as one of themselves.

Occasions will arise when your help will be needed. The star of your story, Jack Robinson, suddenly insists that he cannot read a speech as written. The words don't flow, he feels.

"Change it," says the director, knowing that Jack will sulk himself into a bad performance that day unless the place in the script where it says, "I'll meet you at 7:45, Cynthia," is altered to read, "I'll be there at quarter of eight, honey." If Jack wants a more drastic change, and you are on hand to save the director the trouble of struggling with it himself, to take the star's suggestions and rewrite the speech with the least possible damage to its content, you are, of course, doing yourself and your work a favor as well as accommodating the director. And—it is just possible that the star knows what he is talking about, and that his insistence on a change will inspire you to improve the writing.

During production the director may discover that the picture (its running time estimated to the second by the script clerk) is going to be too long for its fifty-four minutes (without commercials) on television. A page and a half must be cut from the script. You examine the pages still to be shot and, working against time, decide where you can cut out the necessary scenes or scene fragments and still retain coherence and continuity. This kind of thing can always be done—it *has* to be done—but the operation should be performed by the person most familiar with the script, the writer who has lived with it ever since he or she dreamed up the character of the disturbed fireman Jack Robinson is now playing. If you, the writer, aren't around when these emergencies occur, then the emergency will be met by less skillful hands. Those two superfluous minutes will be cut out. If you are absent, you have only yourself to blame when the cutting turns out to be butchery instead of surgery.

The emergency in reverse is more serious. The discovery is suddenly made that the picture is going to be too short if an added scene is not instantly forthcoming. If there is no writer present to invent last-minute dialogue, the collaboration of director, actors, and script girl can be too painful to contemplate.

Your presence on the set, your willingness to help even though your deal doesn't require it, the reputation for dependability you will get by such assistance—these things will weigh in your favor to a degree that may surprise you when the producer of this program has another writing assignment to give out, or when you submit your next story to him. . . .

A recurrent theme in this book is the presence of exceptions to every rule. You never write CUT TO except when ——; never concentrate exposition except in the case of ——; Ibsen's preparation was masterly except for ——.

I am about to sound the theme again, as I reveal that a writer is not always welcome at the scene of the shooting.

This happens (not often) when the producer or the director or an influential star, or perhaps all three, doesn't want the writer of the script around. They have the curious and perverse notion that they themselves can best solve any problem in the writing region. They know exactly what they want, and they resist the threat of the writer making suggestions which may be at variance with their own ideas.

When I became story editor for the television program *Four Star Playhouse,* the first picture I worked on was a half-hour comedy about David Niven's adventures with a psychopathic horse. Niven was not only the star of the films he made for this series, he was also the producer, and he owned part of the company. His was a position of some authority.

On the first day's shooting of this horse farce, Niven drew me aside and pointed a finger. "Who," he asked intensely, "is that fella over there with the green face?"

Since the lighting on the set cast a glaucous pallor over everyone, I had difficulty spotting the fella. But I decided he meant the writer of our script (whom he had never met) and said so.

"Get him out of here!" ordered the producer-star.

I complied, and pondered. This truculent attitude towards the inoffensive author was a puzzler. It was way out of character for Niven, from what I had observed. He was usually friendly, chatted with everybody at the studio, and was probably the most popular member of the Four Star organization. Nor was his relationship with his fellow workers confined to the cheery greeting: an understanding man, he was sensitive to the problems of others and wanted to help solve them.

Another Profession

One grey Monday morning, an absolutely brand-new director prepared to start shooting one of Niven's films for the *Playhouse* program. His name was Richard Kinon, and although this was his directorial debut, he was well known on the lot: he had been a script clerk at Four Star for several years. His ambition was no secret, and David, after consulting his partners, Dick Powell and Charles Boyer, decided to let Kinon try his hand directing a picture improbably titled *Here Comes the Suit.*

At seven forty-five on that first morning, every eye was on Dick Kinon. The company was friendly but curious. They wondered whether Dick would pull it off or fall on his face. Aware of the scrutiny, Dick wondered too. Could he impose a director's authority on his pals? When David arrived from his dressing room, made up for his part, he sensed Dick's nervousness, and at once set about curing it.

"What we'll do," said David privately to the neophyte, "is have a fast rehearsal of this scene before you shoot it." He thumbed through his copy of the script. "Here—in the middle of my speech at the top of Page Two—when we get to that, you stop me and tell me you don't like the way I'm reading it. Ask me to put more emphasis *here.* I shall listen meekly and obey implicitly. That'll show our chums who's the boss, they'll respect you and leap to do your bidding, and from there on in, it should be roses all the way."

And it was. *Here Comes the Suit* was the first of scores of telefilms Dick Kinon has directed in his successful career.

Why should the wise and compassionate Niven storm and pull rank when a writer came on the stage? I found the answer as I became better acquainted with him.

First of all, Niven is a writer himself, as readers of his sprightly autobiography titled *The Moon Is a Balloon*, published in 1971, can readily testify. As a writer, he frequently tinkered with his Four Star scripts, adding lines, touching up the dialogue, changing this, and editing that. He took enormous satisfaction in his contributions. But since he was a writer and, as I have said, a sensitive man, he knew perfectly well that other writers take a dim view of actors rewriting their lines. If changes must be made, the writer likes to have the necessity explained to him and then make the alterations himself. David dreaded the possibility of a strange writer secreting himself on the set, overhearing dialogue that never came from *his* typewriter, and suddenly jumping out at him to demand an explanation. . . .

Sometimes the most effective rewriting is done by merely changing a word or two. David's most remarkable moment as an impromptu writer was inspired by our television sponsor who was shocked at a speech written by P. G. Wodehouse. David played the title role in a dramatization of Wodehouse's short story, *Uncle Fred Flits By*. Some of you will recall that Uncle Fred, otherwise Lord Ickenham, is a demoniac peer who varies a placid country life by periodic forays to London, where he always creates havoc for himself and his nephew, Pongo, by his passion for lunatic practical joking.

At one point Uncle Fred engages in the wholesale character assassination of a respectable but stuffy suburban family, who oppose the romance of two nice young people. Having related the (totally imaginary) crimes of two pillars of the household, Lord Ickenham turns his attention to another relative, Cousin Alf Robbins. He says blandly: ". . . while the jury were probably compelled on the evidence submitted to them to give Cousin Alf Robbins the benefit of the doubt when charged with smuggling dope, everybody knew that he had been doing it for years. I am not blaming him, mind you. If a man can smuggle cocaine and get away with it, good luck to him, say I."

This phoney revelation unsettles the other characters. It unsettled our sponsor, too. Since he footed the bills for the program in the interests of advertising, he also read the scripts. He was late reading this one. Only on the second day of shooting did I get a wire from his New York office, sternly forbidding us to mention the words "dope" or "cocaine" in any picture of his.

Since ignoring this command meant that he wouldn't put up the money for the picture, I hastened to the stage. Roy Kellino, the director, was about to shoot the very scene in which Uncle Fred makes his crowning disclosure of vice in Suburbia. Without comment, I shoved the wire at David and Roy. David looked distraught and said, "Let's not panic."

After a moment he brightened.

"I'm about to make you all very proud of me," he announced. "I shall improve the scene and do exactly what the sponsor asks, at one and the same time. And with only the slightest touch of rewriting. We'll drop the word 'dope,' and the word 'cocaine,' and for them we shall substitute ——"

He told us what he was going to substitute.

The amended dialogue was delivered as follows: ". . . while the jury were probably compelled on the evidence submitted to them to give Cousin Alf Robbins the benefit of the doubt when charged with smuggling—" here David raised his eyebrows suggestively "—you-know-what, everybody knew that he had been doing it for years. I am not blaming him, mind you. If a man can smuggle—" David leered directly into the camera "—*you-know-what* and get away with it, good luck to him, say I."

Uncle Fred went on the air with David delivering the "rewritten" speech in a close-up. The scene had an added element of what can only be described as mysterious indecency.

A Trio of Types

You will be associated with several different kinds of directors if you achieve a career as a television or movie writer.

The first kind is brilliant. He will annoy you intensely by contributing scenes and characterizations without consulting you. You are depressed because the additions are so good. You should have thought of them yourself. You can try to cheer up by telling yourself you are receiving a valuable lesson in humility, that you are enjoying the privilege of watching a master at work, that exposure to genius in action will make your own writing better. None of this will help much, writer ego being what it is. For your peace of mind, this specimen is a very rare bird indeed. Not often will you be overwhelmed by genuine creative dictatorship.

Another type is at the opposite pole. He is a fellow of technical facility. He is competent, and knows what he is doing. He covers every scene with an adequate number of shots. He has an agreeable personality, and is very popular on the set because he doesn't demand tedious rehearsals from the actors, is content with normal, unimaginative camera lighting, and asks nothing more from his professional day than that its close will see the requisite amount of film duly exposed and on its way to the laboratory for processing.

He can tell when an actor is giving a really bad performance, and will doubtless do something to correct it; but he can not, or will not bother to, distinguish between good and mediocre. Good enough is good enough for him.

As for the script—well, that's the writer's department, isn't it? You give it to him, he'll shoot it. He fabricates enthusiasm at the start of the production because that way he needn't bother spending time going over the script with the writer and making changes. Easy does it.

When you find yourself associated with one of these mechanical marvels, give extra special attention to your script. Look it over, yet another time, with the dedicated editorial eye. You will get no help from him, so leave nothing to chance. If there is an element in your teleplay that you feel needs emphasizing over and above the written directions, then emphasize it to him verbally. He will do as you ask. It is easier than arguing with you.

Praise God, there is a third type. He is reasonably talented, reasonably conscientious, reasonably creative. Somebody, quite probably, very like yourself.

The first thing you will notice, when you start working with a director of this class, is that he is as concerned as you are with the problem of turning your story into a good picture. He will want to prepare the script with you, just as he wants to rehearse his actors thoroughly, or discuss matters of lighting and angles with the cameraman (or Director of Photography to give him his correct, but only formally used, title.)

This director will ask for your company when he "walks the sets."

This term means scrutinizing the locations, indoors and out, where the picture is to be shot. You may find that a certain setting, put up by the art department, is different from the background you pictured in your mind when you wrote the scene. You discover that the art director has generously thrown in an unexpected circular staircase in that main hall set. (A realistic note: the staircase has been built for another picture and can be used in yours without additional expense.) You and your director decide to employ the stairs to advantage: you alter a dialogue scene so that the characters pass up and down the steps, and some desirable movement is introduced into a passage that always threatened to be a bit dull because it was all talk and no action.

Another suggestion comes when you see the garden at the back of the house for the first time. You have shown your outlaw hero bursting out of the kitchen door, racing across the garden, and vanishing into the woods a jump ahead of the vigilantes. But there is a high wall around the garden, as it turns out. The wall offers a chance to complicate the flight and give it additional suspense, as the hero struggles to climb over the wall and barely makes it in time. With the director, you work out the mechanics of the change.

I wrote a television picture called *Longhair,* which opened with General Custer disembarking from a river boat at New Orleans. As he stepped ashore, an attempt was made on his life. There was a moment of confusion, and then the unsuccessful assassin disappeared into the crowd, eluding capture. Because I had envisioned a confined landing platform at the foot of the gangplank as the setting, there wasn't a great deal to the attack on Custer: merely a flurry of excitement in a limited space as the hurled knife missed him, some running around, and the announcement by an officer that the lad who was after Longhair's scalp had made good his escape. My envisioning was too modest. We found we could use a huge wharf with mountains of cotton bales piled about, and a stretch of water in a tank, on two sides of the wharf, to simulate several cubic feet of the Mississippi. This all took up half of a large sound stage. The director said tentatively, "We could have quite a chase in this layout," and so we did. We rewrote the scene to introduce much more action. Troops raced after the would-be murderer who kept turning stacks of cotton bales over on them. To top things off, instead of showing him disappearing into the waterfront crowd, we had him dive over the side of the wharf and swim to safety.

Of course, you can run into the reverse situation. You discover you have been too expansive in one place in your script: you have invented some spectacular business that isn't going to work because the tycoon's spacious office you described turns out to be more like a hall bedroom. Here is where our director bails you out. He helps you devise substitute action which can be played in the small set without damaging your story.

He will want to sit down with you and go over the script, page by page, line by line, probably reading it aloud with you. As a result, an occasional awkward line that has slipped by will be improved. He will discuss at length some segment of the script, to be sure that he understands all the implications, and frequently his questions will release ideas for strengthening dramatic or comedy impact here and there. His familiarity with the actors who have been cast in your teleplay will often suggest improvements—or unforeseen but essential changes. For instance—"Chuck Davis is one of the best mimics in pictures. This bit on page 25—where you have Bill imitate that one line of the Commodore's—it's good but I think you could extend it. If you have him do the next speech the same way, it's a sure laugh. Chuck can do it to perfection." And so a scene that would get a quiet chuckle, as originally written, becomes a comedy high spot.

Or—"You'll have to do something about this scene where Jack Robinson comes down the firehouse pole with the cat on his shoulder. Jack has a pathological terror of cats. We'd better make it a hamster."

It is not being too optimistic to say that your chances of getting this kind of director for your maiden teleplay are excellent. His salt-of-the-earth services exist in some abundance. He is in demand, and therefore he is to be found working at most studios. Producers know they need him. They would not stay in business long if all they had to depend on were the geniuses and the hacks.

The Fourth Type

Since this book proposes to help equip you for the real world of television, and because this world has about it nothing of the ivory tower, and because we must take heed of blunt facts even when we are absorbing bland theory, it is necessary to reveal the existence of a fourth kind of director. He represents the smallest group of all, thank goodness. He is a hybrid. He combines the lack of talent and lack of imagination characteristic of the second or mechanistic variety with the zeal and energy of our third and satisfactory type. The spectacle of him in action is deplorable. He is not lazy. He is not indifferent. He is eager to contribute to the script before he shoots it, and his contributions all turn out to be bad. He wants to substitute hackneyed lines for your dialogue, alter your characters so they become the stereotypes he admires, and he suggests inventing a situation for the climax which he knows will be great because he has used it in three other pictures and it always works. This dynamic bundle of tastelessness is not too prevalent, but sooner or later you will run into him if you work in television. (His reputation is such that he is hardly ever found directing feature pictures whose greater rewards are forthcoming only for proven talent.) When you do find yourself working with this fellow, regard his every suggestion with a highly critical eye, learn to say "No!" and if he insists on changes that will obviously damage your teleplay, do not hesitate to appeal to the producer for support. (That support may or may not be forthcoming, but you will have done your best to preserve your integrity and your script.)

Despite the wide variety of directorial characteristics, the partnership between writer and director is an integral part of writing for any dramatic medium. As a novelist, you would have a similar but limited relationship with your editor. But, you see, in writing fiction the words on the page are the end. In writing a teleplay they are only the means. The words are the goal in the creation of a book. They are only the first step on the journey when you create a story to be told in images, a movie to be seen on television.

VII

Writing for Actors

If the director is the most important person to *you* in the process of transferring your story to the screen, you and he are involved with a third person more important than either of you to the audience. This is the actor.

Usually, the person who has just seen an hour of televised romance will be able to tell you the name of the guest star who played the leading role. He will *not* be able to tell you who wrote the teleplay or who directed it. Writer and director are irrelevancies to the average spectator: the story reached him through the agency of the player. He identifies your story, therefore, with the person who brought it to him, who was responsible for the impression it made on him. The actor was good, therefore the impression was good. If your audience thinks about the picture further, they will deduce that the actor was good, in addition to his own talent, because his part was good.

Because his part was good . . . .

The skilled professional writer never lets himself forget the actor's importance. In 1926, a leading American playwright wrote:

> For me, the actor is the only theatrical element who matters. . . . Of all those concerned in the production of a play, only the actor utilizes his talents to their fullest . . . And the dramatist—what, after all, is he but a vicarious actor who happens to write well enough to be useful to real actors? . . . Very few men of literary genius have written plays . . . The drama does not spring from a literary impulse but from a love of the brave, ephemeral, beautiful art of acting . . . The real merit of any play lies in the depth and scope of its acting parts far more than in its story or writing or idea content . . .

Thus the late Sidney Howard in the preface to his play, *Lucky Sam McCarver*. Allowing for high-spirited exaggeration, and mentally noting that we don't much care for his implied downgrading of the writer, we should take to heart what Howard says of the connection between a play's merit and its acting parts. Because from *Hamlet* to *Saint Joan* there has never been a great play that did not have great acting parts. The rule is constant, too, no matter how experimental the drama mediums tend to become. With all its deliberate anachronisms, the history-spanning *The Skin of Our Teeth* presented in Mr. Antrobus and his family and their maid who turns into a beauty queen roles of impressive scope and theatrical effectiveness. *Tiny Alice*, exciting or merely preposterous, has in the unfortunate Julian one of the most arresting parts for an actor since Marlon Brando played Stanley Kowalski in *A Streetcar Named Desire*.

Literally, the writer of teleplays has no contact with actors until his work is finished and polished and ready to be cast, and perhaps not even then if his producer and director choose not to consult him about the selection of players. But it is almost impossible for the experienced writer not to have *somebody* in mind from the very beginning when his characters and their destinies begin to take the shape of a plot. As he ponders the circumstances that are to surround his heroine, a nymph with a sense of humor, the heroine in his mind's eye starts to look like Jane Fonda. The elderly man whose affection for her is more than avuncular begins to sound like Cary Grant.

This daydreaming side of the creative function can be usefully put to work: it is almost invariably easier to write an effective theatrical character if you have somebody specific in mind whom you see moving through the actions of your character and hear speaking your lines. You will discover this for yourself if you write for a series with established characters played by actors whose personalities and mannerisms you know well. These people almost write themselves. You will be rewarded with a similar facility in character creation if you do some imaginary casting of your own characters. This casting is not realistic. It is one of your private, personal construction tools. And if you have conceived a fat sardonic villain with an evil twinkle in his eye you can find it helpful to visualize the late Charles Laughton as you compose his dialogue. Or if you are writing about a Limehouse crook, you might see Peter Sellers going through his paces. The fact that when your story reaches the screen, the Limehouse crook is played by Spencer Spelvin fresh from an actors' workshop on Santa

Monica Boulevard is not significant; what is important is that your fantasizing has resulted in your presenting Mr. Spelvin with a dimensional role of a calibre that Peter Sellers might very well play.

Reality and Consistency

You have read in the first chapter, "To tell your story . . . you must rely on what your characters are seen to do and what they are heard to say." What they are seen to do, their actions, need not detain us long. Physical behavior should correspond to their stations in life, their temperaments, and their ages. In motion, as in speech, they should be consistent. One of the more memorable mistakes of the 1964 television season occurred in a picture about two elderly people, played by Lillian Gish and Walter Pidgeon, both of whom were born before the turn of the century. In one scene Miss Gish retreated into a world of fantasy and playfully leaped off a pier into a lake, to be followed by Mr. Pidgeon in a running dive. He sped to her side and swam with her to shore. The sequence was not, of course, supposed to be realistic. But neither was it supposed to be ludicrous.

Dialogue must be consistent, too, in keeping with the personality of the character. Mark Twain said it a long time ago in the essay that dismembered James Fenimore Cooper's literary style: a rule of literary art requires "that when a personage talks like an illustrated, gilt-edged, tree-calf, hand-tooled, seven-dollar Friendship's Offering in the beginning of a paragraph, he shall not talk like a Negro minstrel in the end of it." If in your first act you establish a character who is sullen and withdrawn, who has difficulty in expressing himself, who is actually only semiarticulate and answers questions in monosyllables, then he must not burst into a flood of eloquence at the climax, no matter what revelations your story calls on him to disclose. Faithfulness to his limitations demands that he give his information haltingly, clumsily, perhaps in response to patient questioning, anything but fluently. Nor should a timid, retiring professor of bacteriology who is afraid of girls suddenly deliver lines suitable for a Casanova bent on overcoming maidenly scruples; not unless you have stuck yourself with a plot which has the professor hit over the head, thereby undergoing a radical personality change.

Television in the United States hews to a pattern of naturalistic dialogue. Most scripts deal with contemporary themes in contemporary settings, and their characters are supposed to sound like the man in the street, or the man on the judge's bench, or the man in the classroom, or the man on a secret mission for the C.I.A., or whatever man in whatever environment you are bringing to life. The ideal is to have your characters sound natural: what they say should sound "true to life."

Achieving this is not always easy. It is possible in a theatrical medium to be too true to life. A genuine conversation recorded on tape is startling to hear: it is full of false stops and starts, incoherencies, repetitions, emphasis on trivialities, and failure to put emphasis on important points. Being too painstakingly accurate can make your dialogue dull and garbled. The majority of professional dramatists steer a satisfactory middle course between chaotic natural speech and literary fluency. Their characters use colloquialisms, their sentences are occasionally unfinished, they sometimes hesitate or start to say something and then stop and rephrase the thought; but these dialogue characteristics are economically employed, just a bit once in a while, to keep the illusion of everyday speech. And if you stop and study the speeches carefully, you find the speakers almost without exception will seem to have their thoughts better marshaled, and are able to express them more readily, than are you and I and the people we meet every day.

Once in a while a talented playwright will achieve a reputation by an unusually concentrated use of everyday speech. Two dramatists who come readily to mind have both written for television and motion pictures: Paddy Chayefsky, who began his career by writing television plays in New York, and the English Harold Pinter, whose prominence derives from television and movie scripts (radio, too) as well as from *The Caretaker* and other stage pieces. The former's classic *Marty* reproduced the speech of New York with uncanny faithfulness; it sounded as if it *had* been recorded on tape, yet so meticulously, so expertly did Chayefsky adapt it that he gave this tenement talk poetic beauty and a lyric texture. The same impressive use of common speech characterized his later play for the stage, *The Tenth Man.* Another Chayefsky teleplay, *A Catered Affair,* even though it was widely admired, illustrates the danger of approaching too close to truly realistic speech: much of the *Affair* dialogue is so authentic that it seems dull, and we become impatient with the all-too-accurate reproduction of gabble.

A Disintegrating Language

Harold Pinter's plays for television have been produced in London on the government-sponsored BBC and also on the commercial channel, Associated Rediffusion. Pinter has hit upon a very strange combination of elements in his plays: their stories generally concern purposely unsolved mysteries, unnamed threats that hang over his characters, and he narrates them in a duplication of real life speech that, in its crudities, repetitions, drabness, transcends Chayefsky's naturalism. A generous lacing of comedy goes into these plays, they are hilarious at the moments they are not inspiring gooseflesh, and while they belong to the Theater of the Absurd they have been accepted by mass audiences and must be considered popular entertainment. Martin Esslin, a BBC producer and writer who coined Theater of the Absurd as a term for the avant garde theater of the 1950's, believes that everyday speech, duplicated on stage or screen as it is by Pinter, leads to the irrationality which is the hallmark of much of today's experimental drama. He writes in his book, *The Theatre of the Absurd* (published by Anchor Books, 1961):

> . . . there is no real contradiction between a meticulous reproduction of reality and a literature of the Absurd. Quite the reverse. Most real conversation, after all, is incoherent, illogical, ungrammatical, and elliptical. By transcribing reality with ruthless accuracy, the dramatist arrives at the disintegrating language of the Absurd. It is the strictly logical dialogue of the rationally constructed play that is unrealistic and highly stylized. In a world that has become absurd, transcribing reality with meticulous care is enough to create the impression of extravagant irrationality.

Harold Pinter is a sharply defined example of the writer for the drama (his kind is fairly profuse in Britain today but extremely rare in the United States) who regards all its channels with respect and whose best work has been done for radio (*The Dwarfs* in 1961) and television (*The Collection*) as well as for the stage (*The Caretaker*) and the theatrical screen (his motion picture scripts based on the novels, *The Pumpkin Eater* and *The Servant*). Entirely too many modern American drama writers regard the stage as the only showcase for their truly serious work and have a patronizing attitude towards television which they find useful as a medium in which they can palm off sloppy, second-rate work for ready money. The fact that American broadcasters are notedly inhospitable to experimental drama, as opposed to the British Broadcasting Company and even England's commercial network, has shaped the attitude of America's playwrights. To date most American broadcasters and advertisers confine any experiments in the Absurd to the television commercials.

As a guide to natural-sounding dialogue that advances your teleplay, you will find it valuable (again) to read popular modern plays for models. There are innumerable published plays that skillfully blend the realistic and the theatrical. Television scripts which do the same thing are usually difficult to come by. Williams, Inge, Miller can be recommended. I would also call your attention to two naturalistic plays of American life by Frank Gilroy, *The Subject Was Roses* and *Who'll Save the Ploughboy?* The drama shelves of any public library will yield many more.

Literary Dialogue

It is important to remember the distinction between literary speech —conversations in novels and short stories—and theatrical speech— that written to be spoken. It is especially important if you have a background of fiction writing. It is not so much that speech in modern fiction is stilted or unreal, but that the dialogue is extended in a manner that is unsuited to films or stage. The speeches are just too long. I pick at random a modern novel called *The Devil's Chapel* by Laurence Lafore (Doubleday) and turn to a scene wherein the heroine is talking to a young Anglican priest she met that morning. Her family has obliquely warned her against him, and the priest asks if she knows of any reason why they should have cautioned her. This is her reply, uninterrupted. Let's look at it in the typographical pattern of a teleplay script:

```
No, I don't. And as you see, I
don't believe they have any
reasons--at least none that
are worth anything--or else,
obviously, I shouldn't be walking
with you and telling you all this.
```

```
To tell you the truth I don't really
know very much about them, or their
motives, let alone their views on
religion. I've not seen them at
all for eight years, and even before
that I hadn't seen much of them.
My sister married when I was eleven.
Clothier--my brother-in-law--
came from Llanbrynmall, but I
barely knew him except as one of
her admirers. Then they moved to
an apartment in town, and they had
their own friends and only came out
to Sunday dinner once or twice a
month. I was never at all close
to them. I do think, though, that
they've changed greatly. And so--
          (she added bleakly)
--has Douglas. I remember him as
being quite a nice child, when he
was six. He isn't at all nice now.
To be quite frank I find them all
changed for the worse. But then
I've changed too, and I've had
rather a difficult time, so I may
also have changed for the worse.
I'm sure they think so.
```

This speech may be acceptable as talk in a novel where its only function is an expository one, but if we were to hear the lady mouth this uninterrupted dialogue on the screen, I'm afraid we should dismiss her as a compulsive talker. Almost everything is wrong with this passage of dialogue from the theater's point of view, beginning with its unnatural length. It rambles. It is undramatic, dealing only with a bland and undefined suspicion. It does not reflect the character of the speaker. It is not even very important since the reader already knows the information the heroine is imparting to her clerical friend. One can only imagine the strain it would put on the actor who must listen quietly and register interest in this torrent of talk from his companion. It is no reflection on the author's talent as a novelist to say that this speech is precisely the kind of thing you must avoid in writing screen or television dialogue.

Shaped for the Screen

Even the speeches in a revered literary classic must be edited and altered for screen presentation. A number of years ago the British produced some admirable film versions of Charles Dickens' novels, the most popular in America being *Great Expectations.* It was followed in the 1940's and 1950's by *Nicholas Nickleby, A Christmas Carol, Oliver Twist,* and *Pickwick Papers.* In common they all possessed wonderful faithfulness to the originals. The characters came to life and were as we had always imagined them, and we recognized familiar lines and expressions spoken by Scrooge and Pip and Sam Weller. But a comparison of the dialogue in the screenplays with that in the books reveals a radical process of editing. Speeches had to be cut or rephrased or condensed and were often completely rewritten. The "faithfulness" was preserved by a fine-comb selection of single lines and colorful phrases lifted from speeches that sometimes took up an entire book page. The essence, not the substance, was put on the screen. If the motion pictures had been literally faithful and duplicated the dialogue of the novels, we should have been bored to distraction. As it was, we were enchanted by what *seemed* to be the re-creation of the stories in visual form.

Therefore—the long speech must be avoided in teleplays, except in a rare instance where it may be justified. Unless, for instance, your leading character is Justice Charles Evans Hughes who, asked to give an opinion, does so.

Nevertheless, you will reach spots in your stories where it is necessary to have a character give the audience vital information, as we have seen in the chapter on exposition and preparation. Shun the temptation to give it to them all at once from the lips of one character so you can get on with the story. Break it up. Back-and-forth dialogue is a prime element of conflict, and conflict is the lifeblood of the theater.

Let us imagine a scene in which one of our characters, Gerald, rushes into his house to break a shocking piece of news to his wife, Ingrid. Now an amateur who had a story to tell, but who lacked knowledge of the dramatic terms in which to tell it, might produce something like the following:

```
                GERALD
     Ingrid! A terrible thing has
     happened. The baby's disappeared.
     He must have been kidnapped. I had
     him with me in the front seat of
                (MORE)
```

```
                GERALD (CONT'D)
the car, and I stopped at the
supermarket to get that can of
corn syrup you wanted. Well, I
wasn't inside more than three
minutes, but when I came out he
was gone. I know he didn't wander
away because I had him strapped in
with the seat belt, and you know he
can't undo it by himself. And the
seat belt wasn't just unfastened--
it had been cut. I called the police
right away and they came--they're
over at the market now. They said
they'd come on over here to the house
in just a few minutes. They want to
talk to you and they said they want
to question me some more. They said
something about giving me a lie
detector test. Can you imagine?
Me? As though I'd had something to
do with it.
```

In addition to the improbability of any mother refraining from interruptions while her husband intones this saga of catastrophe, it is most unlikely that any human being could express himself in such coherent, if undistinguished, prose within a few minutes of a shattering experience. An actor would find it impossible to read this supremely unrealistic speech with any conviction. In real life breaking the horrid news to a mother would undoubtedly be pandemonium. It is the writer's task to suggest chaos, but at the same time to keep the revelation lucid and the uncontrolled reactions of the staggered parents within the bounds of dramatic coherence. The key to a realistic depiction is to give the wife something to say:

```
                GERALD
I don't know--how to tell you
this--the baby--he's--

                INGRID
Oh, my God! He's been hurt!

                GERALD
He's gone--vanished--I don't
know how--I left him in the
car--

                INGRID
Alone?
```

```
                    GERALD
          For three minutes. I parked at
          the market, went inside. When
          I came out--

                    INGRID
          He must have wandered away. Did
          you--

                    GERALD
          He was strapped in his seat belt--

                    INGRID
          He could have unfastened--

                    GERALD
          Ingrid--the belt was cut.

                    INGRID
          The police. We've got to call--

                    GERALD
          I called them. They got there
          right away. They'll be over here
          in a few minutes. They want to
          talk to both of us.

                    INGRID
               (dazed--to herself)
          He's been--kidnapped . . . .
```

This back-and-forth dialogue gives us the facts we need, at the same time it expresses the confusion natural to such a situation. Sentences are unfinished as they would be in real life, but unlike a constantly interrupted passage in real life the ground is rapidly covered and we get to the point sooner. As well as dividing up the long speech, you will notice that I have rearranged some things and omitted nonessentials. Realistically, the husband might very well mention that he went into the market for a can of syrup, but the reference has no place in the kind of theatrical excitement we are concocting. Who cares whether the infant was able to unfasten the seat belt by himself? The point we want to make is that the belt was severed, sinister indication of an abduction. The most arresting word spoken by either Gerald or Ingrid is "kidnapped." We should not lead off with it, but save it until the finish of the scene. Let Ingrid speak the word as the awful truth of what has happened makes itself felt.

Tacked on to Gerald's long speech is a separate element of story progression: his mention of the lie detector test. This most certainly does not belong in a scene exclusively devoted to the announcement of a kidnapping. It is obviously important because of the implication that the police, for reasons as yet unrevealed, are wondering if Gerald had anything to do with his child's disappearance. It must be saved and used to the best possible advantage. I imagine it would be most effective if we were to employ it as the next crisis in the teleplay. The police would arrive at the house, and we would build a scene between them and the parents. Questioning by the detectives would gradually establish that they suspect Gerald for some reason, and the climax of the scene would be their request that Gerald submit to a lie detector test.

Name Dropping

As you write lines for actors, steer clear of the constant use of your characters' names in the speeches. This may sound to you like an absurdly unnecessary caution, in a class with "Be sure you spell the words of your dialogue correctly," but the fact is that the majority of amateur writers, and a surprising number of professionals, tend to tangle themselves in this vexing little booby trap. There is nothing quite like the excessive use of first names to make lines sound unnatural and to infuriate the actor who is trying to memorize them:

"I've been thinking, Ruth—"

"Yes, John?"

"About what Arthur said you did. Ruth, it must have been an exaggeration."

"An exaggeration? It was a falsehood, John, a wicked, out-and-out lie!"

"Thank goodness, Ruth! You don't know what a load you've taken off my mind."

That was John talking to Ruth.

The rationale for this dreadful kind of writing is twofold. It is a hangover from writing for radio, when a listener following a soap opera had to know who was speaking to whom; hence the reiteration of names to avoid the audience's suspecting that a mysterious stranger had entered the scene somewhere along the line and was being addressed. Old timers, who have written millions of words of radio plays, find this name-mentioning a habit hard to break. But it perplexingly crops up among younger writers who have never heard *The Whistler* or *Portia Faces Life,* much less written for them. I believe it stems from a sense of insecurity about the writers' characters and their dimensions. The writers worry lest the personalities of the people they are creating are not projecting. The reiteration of names is an automatic attempt to keep the characters in focus, to shore up their identities. If you keep mentioning somebody's name he seems more real to you.

We don't keep mentioning the names of the people we are talking to in real life. Don't do it in your teleplays.

Unnecessary Directions

The only people who have egos as big as writers' are actors. Their *amour propre* should be borne in mind when you are writing for actors: such consideration will keep the peace and, more important, save time and money.

Almost all actors, when they read their parts, resent a superfluity of directions. A writer, intent on communicating the exact nuances he wishes a scene to possess, will often describe in too explicit detail the manner in which lines should be read. Instead of ignoring this abundance of dialogue directions, or merely taking what seem to him like good suggestions and rejecting the rest, the actor usually responds by working up a hatred for the writer who is arrogantly telling him his business, a hatred that can be responsible for a bad performance. If the lines are any good, he *knows* how they should be read.

Even without reference to the actor, good dialogue should have a minimum of parenthetical directions. If one of your characters hears an explosion, rushes to the window, peers out, then turns to his companions to tell them what he has seen, it is not necessary to write:

```
                PHILIP
           (agitatedly)
      My God! The gas works have blown
      up!
```

The agitation is implicit in Philip's words; you can't blame the actor who plays the part for feeling that his intelligence has been insulted if you tell him that he should read the line in an agitated manner.

But it is frequently necessary to indicate an emotion that is not evident in the words and that may be, indeed, in contradiction to the sense of the speech. A character may be suffering great inward distress, and the audience should know this although the content of what this character says is quite unremarkable. If there *isn't* a direction to indicate the character's state of tension, the danger is that the actor will read the lines in a bland, ordinary way, thus failing to communicate what the author intends. In such a case a parenthetical direction for the dialogue is needed; and after the character's name and just before what he says you insert something like "(barely controlling his feelings)" or "(painfully)" or "(speaking with difficulty)." In other instances an actor may have a line which is innocuous in its meaning but, read correctly, should have sarcastic or reproachful overtones. Thus, the line "I see you're starting to cut down the cherry orchard" should be preceded by "(sarcastically)" or "(reproachfully)."

The best rule of thumb here as elsewhere is to avoid the obvious. If the general tone of delivery is apparent in the lines themselves, leave the details of how to vocalize it to the actor. And if the personalities of your characters have been established by their words and deeds, don't keep reminding the actors of their behavior patterns by writing

```
            OTHELLO
         (jealously)
```

or

```
              IAGO
          (craftily)
```

or

```
            DESDEMONA
          (piteously)
```

I have two other admonitions for you while we are in this slightly tricky area of writing words for people to speak. One concerns tongue-twisters. Most of us would resist the temptation to set down a line like "Douglas is indubitably an infallibly indefatigable fellow," but some little phrases that look perfectly innocent in type raise the very mischief when you try to say them. I remember an actor in a telefilm about Robert Louis Stevenson called *Tusitala* who ruined three takes before mastering the exclamation, "Here comes the Cruiser Keenian!"

He had to shout the news of the ship's arrival very loud and very rapidly, and what he shouted was, "Here comes the Creezer Koonian!"

There is a simple way to keep from lousing up your actors by giving them concealed tongue-twisters: read your dialogue aloud when you finish a scene. It is the only way to expose awkward writing. As well as showing up the treacherous tongue-twister, it reveals an occasional stilted sentence or a patch of purple prose. If you don't feel comfortable articulating a certain line, be assured that the actor who plays the part won't either. I had a student in a recent workshop who read her dialogue to a tape recorder and then played it back, listening to her words with a critical, editorial ear. It's a procedure I recommend, if you have a tape recorder. Otherwise, simply reading your lines aloud will usually be sufficient to secure the effect that painstaking—but silent—editing doesn't always achieve.

The Use of Dialect

My other cautionary note concerns how you handle dialect, what you do about accents. Books have been written by speech experts and dialogue directors on the correct reproduction of dialects. At one end of the spectrum you find the believers in a phonetic, syllable-by-syllable laying out of unusual pronunciations. I tend to think of these authorities as the Uncle Remus School: open one of Joel Chandler Harris's books and you'll find a sentence like "I tuck'n year some flutterments up dar 'mungs de rafters, en I look up, en dar wuz a Bat sailin' 'roun'." The trouble with this kind of writing is that you have to read it twice before you can figure out what Uncle Remus is talking about. And any script whose dialogue has to be read twice by a Hollywood producer has a serious strike against it.

At the spectrum's other end are writers like Lillian Hellman who prefaces *The Little Foxes* with the notation, "There has been no attempt to write Southern dialect. It is to be understood that the accents are Southern."

But although Miss Hellman eschewed the *y'all come git yo' co'n pone* spelling in her play, she took great care by her use of phrases to make her dialogue seem authentically Southern. Poor Birdie, alcoholic and persecuted, speaks in the colloquialisms that could be used only by a Southern belle. But the words of her regional talk are correctly spelled. There is no attempt to literalize the soft slurring of Southern speech by dropped final g's and omitted consonants.

This method I believe to be the most satisfactory approach to dialect. Expressions native to the locale, appearing now and then, give a region's color and flavor far more effectively than the tortured attempt to be totally accurate. The heroine's lines in *Come Back, Little Sheba* are written for the most part in straightforward, impeccable English. Here and there William Inge gives her a "I hafta get busy" or "Doc was sortuva Mama's boy" to indicate that Lola is a slovenly speaker. With these occasional clues to guide her, plus regional expressions, the result in the mouth of an accomplished actress is a fine approximation of pure Midwest Twang.

The great danger in writing dialect phonetically is exaggeration. Actors are creative, and all they require is a colloquialism here and there to enable them to build a good dialogue pattern. But it is extremely difficult for anybody, trying to follow the exact shadings in a too faithfully reproduced speech, not to come up with a heavy accent that tends to burlesque its prototype and be hard to understand. We had an example of the appalling result of dialect laid on with a trowel in a British film of 1963, *Sparrows Can't Sing,* which so faithfully reproduced the accents of London's East End that audiences in the United States found it unintelligible and, after a false start, it was released here with English titles at the bottom of the screen as though it were in a foreign language.

In advising you to use a light hand with dialect, I speak once again from experience. I produced a number of westerns for television in 1960 and 1961, and at an early stage I learned to edit those scripts that were full of "Howdy pardner's" and "Ah reckon 'twon't be long naow's." It is deplorable but true that television actors frequently see their scripts for the first time the day before they play their parts, and as a result they tend to follow most faithfully what is set down in their dialogue. There is no time for the fine shadings that create a consistent character speech. Adherence to the overwritten word means exaggeration. Show a television actor his lines with the Deadwood lingo syllabically spelled out for him, and he will sound as though he's making fun of the part.

Two tips. Stay away from characters who speak brokena Ingleesh.

The day is long gone when the stereotype foreigner was funny. And for goodness' sake, don't write about people whose speech you have never heard. If you are going to use accents, be sure you know how they sound. The result, if you don't, can only be disastrous.

Cataloguing Your Characters

It is standard practice for the writer to include a cast list in the script of a teleplay. Unlike a stage play, which lists its characters in the order of their appearance, a teleplay always presents them according to their importance in the story, which generally means that the character with the most lines, probably the star of the show, comes first. He is followed by characters of diminishing importance, ending up with the "silent bit" parts and then the extras if there are any.

The name of each character on the list is followed by a brief description. It is important that descriptions be accurate, lean, very much to the point. Stay away from fanciful discussions of your peoples' psyches, which might make entertaining reading in a published stage play but are calculated to madden a harassed casting director.

The speed and pressure of television production govern the writer's obligations in outlining his cast. The casting director has only a limited time in which to read the script, suggest to the producer and director actors for the parts, get hold of those actors and have them come to the studio for interviews, and, when the producer makes the final selection, engage them for the parts. In view of the swiftness with which all this must be accomplished, a reliable check list of characters is vital. The casting director should be able to run down the descriptions of characters and make his preliminary listing of possible actors for each part.

The descriptions must emphasize physical appearance. General Taylor is "a tall, heavyset man in his middle forties with a deep voice and a commanding presence." It is unwise to make the description too specific. You see, there are probably five or six good available actors who can play the role of a middle-aged general with an impressive appearance, and it is utterly unrealistic for you to insist in your description of him that he is "partially bald, slightly gray at the temples, has protruding teeth, and a medium-sized paunch." Unless his teeth and his tummy have something to do with the plot (rather unlikely) those picturesque details should be left out, no matter what your private vision of the General is. Your description should be detailed enough to suggest the *kind* of actor who can play the part but sufficiently broad so that more than one good player can be considered. Parenthetically, do not label any of your characters "a Gregory Peck type" or "a Joan Fontaine type" even though you would consider such casting ideal: it is not helpful and it is the stamp of the amateur.

Many writers make up their cast lists from descriptions in the body of the script. A character introduced and described on page 17 will be similarly described in the list at the front of the script. You may find this a convenience: if the description of the character is too long where he appears in the script, you can condense it for the listing.

For cast list purposes a character's function in the script should be mentioned only briefly. I have seen cast lists whose creators were so anxious to picture their people vividly that they practically wrote synopses of the teleplays. They go something like this:

```
ANNIE . . . . . . . . . . . . . Bertha's sister-in-law, a
                                homely woman in her mid-
                                fifties, who hates Bertha
                                because Bertha is more
                                attractive, and deliberately
                                spreads the rumor that
                                Thornton Mayfield is really
                                the father of Willoughby,
                                Bertha's teenaged,
                                handicapped son.
```

It is enough to list Annie as "Bertha's sister-in-law. Plain. About fifty-five."

A word about a series cast list for a show with continuing characters. It is not, of course, necessary to describe the characters who run through all the stories, appearing regularly. You merely list the names of the ones who appear in your teleplay (not every series character has to appear in every film) at the top of the cast. A typical cast list will look like what follows. It is always for obvious reasons inserted at the beginning of the script. We will assume that this one is for a program, with continuing characters, called *Old Judge Palmer*.

CAST LIST

```
JUDGE ROBERT PALMER
ARNIE
ELIZABETH

THERESA PALMER . . . . . . . . . . Judge Palmer's cousin, a
                                   beautiful woman in her late
                                   thirties. Simply but
                                   expensively gowned.

VINEGAR BOTTS . . . . . . . . . . .An ex-pug, about 45, with
                                   a free and easy manner.
                                   Stocky and muscular.

BLAINE BLACKTON . . . . . . . . . .A bearded poet of 26 or so.
                                   Willowy, well-dressed, too
                                   elegant to be a beatnik.

MRS. SINCLAIR . . . . . . . . . . .A thin, elderly, white-
                                   haired widow with a
                                   sarcastic manner.

DR. THROOP (bit part) . . . . . .Dignified professional man
                                   in middle life.

EXTRAS:  audience in movie house, passersby in front of
         Palmer home.
```

Not long ago the producer of a successful, distinguished television show sought the services of a well-known actress to appear as guest star in one of his films. A preliminary phone conversation indicated that the star would definitely be interested in doing the part, and the producer sent her the script. It was returned within a week with a curt refusal, but no comment beyond "I don't feel the part is suitable." Later, the producer found out that the lady had been deeply offended by the script's description of the part she was expected to play. A direction referred to the Countess Velda as "a once beautiful woman on whose face dissipation has etched ugly lines. She has ceased to care about herself, and although her gowns are costly she wears them carelessly and without distinction."

It takes a very perceptive actress indeed to survive the first cold shock of discovering that she is expected to play an old bag, and to read on with a proper appreciation of the part's virtues. The writer might just as well be tactful, thus avoiding this unpleasant and unnecessary risk, and describe Countess Velda as "a striking woman who has lived a rich, full life and in whose face is character as well as beauty."

If you think I am going to whimsical lengths in stressing the sensibilities of actresses, please recall that when Lynn Fontanne starred in *The Visit* by Friedrich Duerrenmatt, its English title had been shortened from the German original, which was *The Visit of the Old Lady*.

VIII

The Writer's World

As we approach the end of the first part of our book (which I have labeled *Chiefly Theory* for your convenience and mine), we have some unfinished business to dispose of before we get into *Chiefly Practice.* One of the matters making up this unfinished business concerns the fact film and its relation to the kind of television writing we have been studying.

Until now your attention has been turned to the elements that go into the writing of television drama. I have emphasized more than once that our concern is with fundamental rules applying to all drama: the stage, motion pictures, radio (although we have had no occasion to examine that diminished art form), as well as television. Plainly, the subject of our text is *fictional* television writing. We have studied the construction of invented television stories. We have ignored, as being outside the scope of this book, the writing and production of news broadcasts and those documentary films which profess to be undramatized recordings of fact. This use of the television medium comes under the heading of journalism and is, of course, a vast and separate subject.

There are three regions, however, where fact films and fiction films impinge on each other in both television scripts and feature screenplays. The most obvious and by far the most important is to be found in the use a writer frequently makes of factual material within the body of his fictional script. His teleplay may be based on or suggested by a topical occurrence, a situation taken from real life.

In Touch with Reality

The television and movie writer is more apt to be in contact with the real world, with the infinite human activities of his time, than the doctor, the physicist, the chemist, or the geologist whose attention is necessarily narrowed for most of his working hours. This looks like a paradox only if you insist on regarding the theater as dealing in unreality, in magic and illusion and escape. It is concerned with these things, of course, but exclusively concerned only in the rare cases of a Peter Pan or a Mary Poppins. Primarily, the theater has always reflected reality, in part or in whole, sometimes faithfully and sometimes in a distorting mirror. Today more than in past times the writer for popular forms must know what is going on around him. If he breaks touch with reality and depends solely on his imagination or, worse still, confuses reality with its depiction in other works of drama or fiction—thinking he is dealing with the real thing when actually he is reworking characters and their plights from an imperfectly remembered movie he saw in 1960—he is seriously impairing his chances of becoming a successful writer for stage, screen, or tube.

The charge is frequently heard that television offers only escapist entertainment. Television is certainly intent on entertainment, and there is no denying that its approach to the problems of the world is something less than profound, but a recent season saw the following subjects treated on "entertainment" shows (there's nothing here from any news or documentary programs): actors blacklisted because of alleged radical records, alcoholism and its consequences, opposition to sex education classes in high school, the tension involved in maintaining morale in a veterans' hospital, the use of narcotics among teenagers, how a prostitute can make a good mother, the plight of a conservative statesman who gets unwelcome support from a neo-fascist group, the case for and against legalized abortion, the discovery by the United States ambassador to the United Nations that the case he is pressing is a tangle of lies devised by his superiors. The point is not that these subjects were handled with kid gloves, or in many instances served for pictures that were superficial and even dishonest. What must impress us is that the writer took reality and did *something* with it. He had to draw on his own experiences, or his knowledge of reported events, and use it as his raw material. The writer must find out exactly what is going on up in Alberta before he can write his story based on the first woman to join the Canadian Royal Mounted Police.

Whatever his field, a writer has to be a researcher. Some of the elementary things you were told when you started to write bear repeating. They are important. They are the rules for beginners, and for the author who has published five novels and the screenwriter whose desk is crammed with produced scripts.

Keep a notebook. Jot down happenings. Record people's traits that catch your interest, even if they fail to suggest stories instantly. They will be usable some day. Do not rely on your memory. If you are only halfway observant, you will see much that you can eventually use in your writing that will slip away if you don't take notes.

Clip the newspapers. A file of newspaper items is inspiration's handmaiden. The ideal clipping is a short piece at the bottom of page 16 which casts an unusual light on the human predicament but isn't so unique, dramatic, or startling that it immediately appeals to every hungry writer looking for story material. Some professional writers avoid the true story that is too good. When the wire services carried the story of the drunken driver who ran over a boy, raced home panic-stricken, and then was found hiding in his attic by the police who informed him it was his own son he had struck and killed, a dozen amateur writers sent story departments scripts and outlines based on the macabre coincidence. But instead of ignoring the news story that is all too obvious dramatic material, the seasoned writer would be wise to put it away for reference in the distant future. The chances are that none of the hasty efforts suggested by fact will sell, and in a year the event will be forgotten and then can be profitably put to work.

The Unseen Speaker

The two other resemblances between fact films and fiction films are technical matters but both are the writer's concern and he must know how to use them in his teleplay. One is the technique of narration, the other the presence of stock shots in the television script.

You have all heard the voice of a narrator coming from the

television screen as you watched the shifting images of a travel film about a journey down the Nile or a voyage around the Aran Islands. Or perhaps the voice interpreted the shots in a documentary dealing with the clouded political situation in the Far East. The pictures projected on the screen would not be entirely understandable without the narration or commentary. Narration is a standard device of the fact film, whether it is a documentary for the movie theater or a picture written for the television tube or screen. The use of narration in fiction films is by no means so common. Nevertheless, it is a perfectly legitimate device in television and motion picture drama provided it is employed most sparingly and only when the conventional technique of combined visualization and speech is not able to provide information as clearly and effectively. Narration is used in teleplays to establish a setting (generally at the beginning of the script) and to tell the audience what they must know about conditions in this setting. Although narration, expertly written and positioned in the script, can sometimes add impressiveness or excitement to a teleplay situation, it is primarily a time-saving device. A few brief shots, with the narrator's voice telling us what is going on can accomplish in two minutes what the more familiar variety of television storytelling—action and dialogue in "acted out" scenes—would take twice as long to make clear.

The typographical appearance of your narration should resemble closely that of an ordinary passage of dialogue. It will be narrowly columned in the center of the teleplay page exactly like a character's speech. The heading, written in capitals, will be NARRATION or NARRATOR or NARRATOR'S VOICE; any of the three is correct. Let us suppose, for an example, that you wish to open your teleplay by imparting important information to the audience concerning your leading characters, the place where they live, and the period in which the events of your story take place. Succinctly, you decide to present your exposition by means of narration. Your first scene, then, will look like this:

```
                                              FADE IN:

EXT. LYNCH FARM    LONG SHOT    DAY

The view is across a succession of fields, set in beautiful
rolling country that stretches away to a range of mountains
rising against a near horizon. Some of the fields are
```

```
planted in corn, tall and waving. After a moment to estab-
lish the lush summer landscape, CAMERA PANS SLOWLY LEFT TO
RIGHT, crossing a pasturage where cattle graze, moving past
the long rambling stables of the Lynch farm, and finally
bringing into sight the white, two-story farmhouse. CAMERA
HOLDS on house. Over this SHOT:

                    NARRATOR'S VOICE
          Three generations of the Lynch family
          have tilled their land in this south-
          ern corner of the Shenandoah Valley.
          The farm laid out by the first Thomas
          Lynch has slowly grown for more than
          half a peaceful century. But time is
          running out and peace must have an
          end. And the year is 1861. Young
          Tom Lynch, the third to bear the name,
          is leaving for the war . . .
```

We are now free to cut to Captain Lynch taking leave of his loved ones before departing to join Ashby's Brigade of the Seventh Virginia Cavalry. In less than a minute of screen time we have set up our locale, identified the family our story will tell about, and indicated that the Civil War is starting. Now attempting to dramatize all this in the beginning of your teleplay (I am assuming that it is information vital for the audience to know at the opening of the story) would result in one of those old-fashioned exposition scenes we heard about in Chapter III, wherein the characters chatter away, telling each other—for our benefit—what all of them unless severely retarded already must know.

In addition to this type of formal narration in which the speaker is impersonal, a detached and disembodied voice, you will find need once in a great while to use an actual character in the teleplay as narrator. You may decide, for instance, that a certain element of your story is essential but uninteresting. It is a plot link, it has to be present, but it lacks warmth and excitement and as an innately pedestrian piece of storytelling it should be stated briefly. Your decision is to allow the character involved to tell about it, to telescope it. Imagine you are writing of one Alan Smith, whose wife has left him and who determines to find her at all costs. At the end of one scene he sets out to look for her. To achieve the best dramatic effect, you would like to go at once to their meeting. But later on it is going to be important for the audience to know that Alan spent three weeks trying to find her. So we must establish here and now that the search was not easy. To show the search, to write it into your teleplay, even in a series of short scenes, will slow everything up; you will run the danger of losing your audience. So you construct a bridge, a bridge of narration, that speedily takes the viewer from the beginning of Alan's quest to its successful conclusion. The bridge will look like the following in your teleplay. We will suppose that Alan finally caught up with his wife, Elizabeth, in a small hotel in Paris.

```
                                               DISSOLVE:


INT. SMALL HOTEL LOBBY    MED. SHOT ENTRANCE    DAY

Alan enters from the street and crosses to the tiny office
of the concierge, CAMERA PANNING WITH HIM. The concierge, a
tall woman with a blank face, emerges from the office and
stares at Alan as he questions her. We do not hear their
voices since there is NARRATION over the SHOT. The concierge
obtains a ledger from her office, consults it and shows a
page to Alan. He nods and starts talking excitedly. Over all
the above we hear

                         ALAN'S VOICE
                For three weeks I had no luck.
                Elizabeth seemed to have vanished
                off the earth. I checked every
                hotel on the Left Bank, including
                the flea bags. No Elizabeth. With-
                out much hope I looked into a place,
                a kind of pension-hotel that took
                women only. It was the last spot I'd
                expect to find my dear wife in. But
                with Elizabeth you never know. She
                had been living here quietly for a
                couple of weeks, the concierge told
                me.
```

That bit of business with its accompanying explanation should last less than a minute. But it has smoothly transported us to the place we had to reach and it has made its point that Alan had to look for a while before he found his wife. Having written this narration bridge, you can return to conventional teleplay technique as you develop your story. You can most easily do this by following the above block of narration with a cut to "CLOSE SHOT ALAN AND CONCIERGE" or simply "ANOTHER ANGLE" and pick up their dialogue as the concierge says she will call Elizabeth's room.

A warning. Before you employ narration in your teleplay, make certain that the points you wish to establish cannot be efficiently made in any other way. Nothing is more glaringly apparent than narration misused. Using it to excess creates the impression that narration is just a crutch for a lazy writer who is refusing to take the time and trouble to write the exposition into his script in a natural and unobtrusive manner (see Chapter III). When it is overworked, that is precisely what narration becomes.

From the Film Library

What is a stock shot? It is a shot or scene which is cut into a motion picture or a telefilm but which has not been expressly shot (filmed, photographed) for that particular movie. It comes from a film library, in most cases, whose vaults contain millions of feet of film on every conceivable subject from a close-up of a humming bird to a head-on collision between locomotives. It is selected by the cutter or film editor whose responsibility it is to insure that the stock shot is a reasonably good match for the staged scenes in the picture with which there is a visual and dramatic connection. To illustrate: you have written a staged scene with your hero standing on a city street and looking across the street at a tall office building. You cut to the building he is staring at. If it is decided to use a stock shot of an actual office building, then that building must look as if it very well could belong on the same street.

Almost any teleplay you examine will contain stock shots. These three are typical:

```
EXT. GERMAN FORT AT CASSINO    LONG SHOT    DAY    (STOCK)

Exploding shells cause geysers of earth and masonry to
erupt as the Americans start to lay down a barrage on the
enemy stronghold.


EXT. MOUNT EVEREST    LONG SHOT    DAY    (STOCK)

Four or five figures roped together, obviously mountain
climbers, are struggling up the side of the celebrated peak.


EXT. INTERNATIONAL AIRPORT    LONG SHOT    NIGHT    (STOCK)

A jet whooshes in for a landing. It is raining and the run-
ways glisten in the wet with reflected lights. SOUND of
tires screeching as the plane barrels down runway.
```

The trio of shots—of warfare, of mountain climbing, of a plane landing—have one thing in common (in addition to the STOCK label, always written in parentheses at the right of the direction heading). They are far too expensive to be included in the average modestly budgeted telefilm. They are too costly, that is, if the director has to recreate the Battle of Cassino on the studio's back lot, or take a camera crew to Mount Everest or even arrange for a jet liner to make a special landing on a rainy night for the benefit of his cameras. These scenes all represent footage derived from newsreels or documentaries or from elaborate, multi-million-dollar feature pictures.

Television programs depend heavily on stock shots because the popular story series are produced as cheaply as possible, or as is commensurate with a certain quality level. Two half-hour shows, both devoted to pictorial surveys of World War I, were entirely comprised of stock footage half a century old at the time they were edited for television showing, assembled from a variety of sources including government archives in Europe and America. These extreme examples of the use of stock footage, of course, belong to the classification of documentaries or fact films. But the producers of many television fiction films, devised solely for entertainment, lean heavily on stock footage to keep expenses down. *Combat,* a successful program about a group of soldiers in World War II, made extensive use of battlefield shots and pictures of sizeable troop movements, artillery duels, and savage infantry fighting, all culled from the motion picture coverage of World War II. A similar television story program, *12 O'Clock High,* its subject the American Bomber Command in England in 1943–44, included hundreds of thousands of feet of Air Force stock (film coverage) of the great bombing raids carried out by the B-17's, familiarly known as Flying Fortresses. The stock shot action sequences in both programs were carefully matched with scenes photographed on exterior locations or studio sound stages. You have undoubtedly seen this kind of stock matching many times. Shot 1 shows a German fighter plane, guns blazing, as it attacks one of the lumbering American bombers. This shot is of course an actual one—a stock shot—filmed in 1943 from a plane in combat. Shot 2 is supposedly the interior of the bomber: this shot, made in the studio, shows our fictional characters as they react to the Messerschmitt's attack. Shot 3 is another piece of stock film in which an actual B-17 starts to fall in flames.

The programs *12 O'Clock High* and *Combat* are specialized cases. Writing for programs like these demands conferences between writer and producer after the former's story has been accepted but before he works it into the detailed teleplay form. The writer must know what stock footage is available before he can construct the specific action of each sequence.

Even the more usual type of television fiction film, in which there is no need for the constant intercutting of stock footage, will almost always include some stock shots. To establish a setting—downtown Manhattan with its skyscrapers at night, the campus of a big university, a Lake Michigan auto ferry docking at Milwaukee—the writer will indicate in his teleplay that these scenes are stock. The stock shot is then succeeded by the next scene (which is not stock) of a cleaning woman in a skyscraper office in the first example; a professor entering a university classroom in the second; our heroine coming down a gangplank after we have seen (in the stock shot) the ferry tying up at the Milwaukee pier. (And put a dissolve between the establishing stock shot and the fictional action that follows to account for any time lapse. There would have to be such a brief passage of time, for instance, between the ferry's arrival and the heroine's disembarking.)

Let us imagine that you find it necessary to include in your teleplay a short sequence in which two of your characters attend the St. Patrick's Day parade in New York City. Here is how you do it and contrive to stay within your program's budget by using only your two principals, a dozen extras, and some stock footage:

```
EXT. FIFTH AVE.    MED. SHOT KELLY AND MULDOON    DAY

Kelly and Muldoon are among the crowd lining the sidewalk
and watching the St. Patrick's Day parade. In this medium
shot twelve other spectators are visible; they are packed
together and, with the aid of crowd noise SOUND, they give
the impression of a huge crowd. SOUND of band music over
crowd noise.

                          KELLY
                There must be twenty-five
                hundred people in this parade.

EXT. FIFTH AVE.    REVERSE ANGLE ON PARADE    (STOCK)

A blaring brass band is passing by. Behind the band march
the members of a social club carrying small flags. Cheering
crowds pack the sidewalks.
```

```
CLOSE SHOT    KELLY AND MULDOON

                         MULDOON
                    (glaring at Kelly)
               Twenty-five hundred! Why man--
               there's at least two thousand!

LONG SHOT    THE PARADE    (STOCK)

Shooting south on Fifth Avenue, showing the parade stretch-
ing down towards Washington Square. Sidewalks packed with
crowds. SOUND of band music, applause, cheering.
```

Inserting stock shots in your teleplay is a simple procedure, really, and should not weigh heavily on your mind. Make use of a stock shot in your script (1) if it is a scene that you vitally need, (2) if it involves so many people and/or such an expensive setting that reason tells you it is impractical (for a television budget) to consider it a scene to be shot specifically for your picture, and (3) if your common sense tells you that it can probably be secured. Most television programs are produced by, or in close cooperation with, major motion picture studios whose film libraries have in their vaults stock shots drawn from newsreels and feature pictures produced over a period of years. Nearly everything on the contemporary scene has been photographed at one time or another, and you need not hesitate to include such (stock shot) scenes in your teleplay as city crowds, snow storms, floods, horse races, burning buildings, the Paris metro, church services, and meetings of the United Nations. I believe we would find it far more difficult to compile a list of subjects for which stock film does *not* exist.

The Set List

Since the need to practice economy affects every phase of television production from the story subject chosen by the writer to the time allotted for shooting his script, and includes as we have seen the wide use of stock footage to keep down the costs of sets and extras, it would be well to emphasize here that you should not write too many different sets, or changes of scene, into your teleplay. You learned in Chapter IV the need to avoid over-elaborate sets in a telefilm because the budget would not permit, and for the same reason you may not have an inordinate number of settings. The production department frowns on too many as well as too much. Sets, both interior and exterior, in the average hour teleplay generally do not exceed twelve: if you can use fewer, and still tell your story effectively, so much the better.

It is customary to list the sets on a separate page at the beginning of your teleplay script. This set list, which comes immediately after the cast list, is there for the benefit of the production supervisor, the head of the production department, who uses it in his preliminary survey of the teleplay. It assists him in much the same way that the cast list does the casting director. (It often happens that a writer is asked to make revisions in his teleplay not because the producer wants the quality of the script improved but because it is necessary to eliminate one or more sets, or consolidate several into one, in order that the picture may be produced within the prescribed budget.) When you have finished your teleplay, go through it carefully and very briefly list each different set. List it only once, of course, even if you return to it several times and play a number of sequences therein. Be sure to include everything, outdoor locales as well as interior sets. If you have used stock shots, list them and label them stock (but they need not be counted among the limited *real* sets you are permitted: if you have used twelve sets that must be built or found on location in your teleplay, the stock shots may be in addition to them).

The page in your teleplay with the set list looks like this:

```
                        SET LIST


EXTERIORS

Garberville Main Street (country town)
The County Court House
Wooded Slope near Garberville
Country Dirt Road
Dr. Miller's House on Residential Street
Train Entering Station (STOCK)
Train Speeding across Bridge (STOCK)

INTERIORS

Dr. Miller's House (living room and dining area)
Bedroom in Mrs. Winthrop's House
Courtroom in County Court House
Deputy's Office
Dr. Miller's Office
Hospital Reception Desk
Hanson's Grocery Store
```

An Assessment

That concludes our survey of the teleplay and how to write it (*except* for some important odds and ends that I shall dispose of in the final chapter of Part Two: I have been forced to deal with so many exceptions posed by our subject that I shall indulge myself with one of my own). The second part of the book deals with matters pertaining to marketing your teleplay. We shall contemplate the writing of an outline which presents your teleplay in brief form without sacrificing its values. We shall discover something about the people you will meet and work with if you adopt television writing as a profession. They include story editors and agents and your fellow members of the Writers Guild. Before we start this section I would like to pause for a page or two and have you think about the connection between what you are learning to do now and the future demands of your profession. If you continue to write for television or the theater screen or both, if you are successful, what kind of life will you be leading? Bluntly—just what are you getting into?

The relationship between learning and work in the theater is an enduring one. It is not a linkage peculiar to the beginning of your career. It will go on just as long as you live and stay faithful to the theater. In very few other professions does a man's work flow into his personal life, become such an inseparable part of it, as it does in this one. Involvement with your work medium is total. If this doesn't impress you as a truly joyful prospect, you should not be a writer of teleplays (or stage plays or movie scripts) but should instantly transfer your efforts to some other area where I should think you would be very successful, considering the tenacity you must possess to have reached this chapter.

The rewards for a devoted drama writer in terms of the daily life he leads, I happen to believe, are enormous. The theater, in all its forms, is his bread and butter, his entertainment and recreation, his hobby, the source of his ever-increasing authority, and his consuming passion.

With what a clear conscience you can amuse yourself! The burdened businessman, the banker and the lawyer, can feel guilty at having spent golden hours watching a Bergman program of *Smiles of a*

Summer Night and *The Magician*. Or at having wasted time looking at *Ben Kronkeit M.D.* on television. This indulgence in entertainment is plain duty in your case. Look at what you're learning to do (in the case of a fine piece of work) and to avoid (if the show is a disaster).

You can cram your life with an enjoyment that is also the acquisition of knowledge. Read plays for relaxation and pleasure. Depending on your mood, the play may be *Mourning Becomes Electra, Dr. Knock, You Never Can Tell, Cat on a Hot Tin Roof*, or *The Good Woman of Setzuan*. Don't confine yourself to the admired semiclassics. Popular trash has its lessons to offer. *Seven Keys to Baldpate, Under Orders, Lightnin', Lulu Belle, White Cargo,* and *The Shanghai Gesture* are hoary hits of yesterday's stage readily available (but not in the academic anthologies) and great fun to read. While you will quickly spot the parts that have dated badly, you may be surprised at their skillful treatment of character and incident. There are many more.

Study the mad history of the movies with its sidewise, crab-like, trial-and-error progress. Read Lewis Jacobs' *Rise of the American Film* for a comprehensive account of the native industry from its origins to the middle 1930's; the *History of Motion Pictures* by Bardèche and Brassillach for a European account of the same time span; Paul Rotha's *The Film Till Now* for a world view.

Build up your background by reading the critics of stage and screen. The first part of *Agee on Film* is a selection of writings on the movies of the 1940's by the late James Agee, possibly the most brilliant critic of the cinema since the youthful André Sennwald of the *New York Times* blew himself up in his Manhattan apartment in 1935. For a more recent survey of the international movie scene, try John Russell Taylor's *Cinema Eye, Cinema Ear* which probes deeply into the pictures of Truffaut, Fellini, Hitchcock, and other contemporary artists. Taylor is an Englishman whose point of view is directed towards the stage, television, and the theater film. His writing reflects the relationship of the three forms, currently much closer in Britain than in this country. His book, *Anger and After* (retitled more attractively but less accurately *The Angry Theater* for publication in the United States), is a detached but perceptive appraisal of those recent developments (the plays and movies and television of John Osborne, Harold Pinter, and company) which now influence the dramatic writing of the west.

For other opinions of the contemporary stage, read the criticism of

Brustein, Bentley, Kerr, and Tynan. Their writings cover a wide field and are often in contradiction. You will find them entertaining, informative, and witty. None of the four is without his crotchets.

Speaking of Crotchets—

There is no more delightful reading than Bernard Shaw's play reviews, written when he was the dramatic critic of the London *Saturday Review* from 1895 to 1898. Whether you read them for the Shavian style, for a record of the British theater of the period, for their uninhibited traducing of Sydney Grundy, Pinero, Jones, and other sacred cows of the late Victorian stage, or for their extraordinary, incisive discussions of dramatic construction, production, techniques of writing, acting, and directing, you will be handsomely repaid.

That period of the late 1890's has significance for us. It was the time when today's theater—as it exists in films and television and the popular, nonexperimental stage—took shape and began to grow. More orthodox as a chronicler of these critical years than Shaw is William Archer whose name has crept into these pages once or twice before. This Scotsman (H. G. Wells said he possessed "an unscrupulous integrity") was an able critic and a meticulous historian who, however, must be read with some reservations. *His* crotchet, at least when he was writing in 1922 towards the end of his life, was his conviction that the English-speaking theater of the day had attained a state of absolute technical perfection. He vastly admired its realism, its naturalistic speech, its abiding resemblance to life as we appear to live it, and he was unable to conceive of any progress beyond the sturdy dramatic architecture developed by such dramatists as Galsworthy and Granville-Barker. Despite his belief that Jerusalem was already built in England's pleasant greenroom, Archer is very much worth reading today for his clear and engrossing documentation of a vital period in the English and, by association, American theaters.

Archer died at precisely the right moment. He had just seen produced his one and only successful play, a rickety but tremendously popular melodrama, *The Green Goddess,* starring the celebrated George Arliss as a wicked rajah. And he made his exit before the arrival in the world theater of Brecht and his contemporaries, the tamperers with all Archer revered . . . .

An agreeable feature of your profession is its attraction for your family and associates, although they themselves may not be productively involved in the theater. Since your business is what the rest of the world calls entertainment, you will have company if you want it in your professional surveys. Your only difficulty may be in escaping the skeptical stare when you allude to theater-going or television-watching as work. But, if spending time in the bosom of your family seems desirable, you are in a better position than most of your fellows. Your partner will contentedly go along on a fortnight's trip to Stratford or Ashland to see some of the Shakespeare season, or to San Francisco for an international film festival, where she or he would stay home if you were bound for a gynecologists' conference or a frozen-shrimp packers' convention.

It is well that there are such compensations in the life of a television writer. For there is a great deal of hard work, too; work that must often be performed under high pressure. The pressure may come from your producer who calls up to announce that he is deeply distressed to hurry you, but there has been a radical change in his shooting schedule and, if disaster is to be averted, you must deliver the first draft of your script this Friday instead of next Tuesday. There is also the pressure that comes from within, when the writer admits to himself that his climax is bland and weak, and faces the fact that he will have to rewrite the entire first act, and inject new elements into his story stream, if he is to correct what is wrong. This internal pressure is more nerve-wracking. Producers can sometimes be argued with and convinced. But the pressure applied by the silent creative voice will not relax until you have carried out its dictates.

PART TWO

CHIEFLY PRACTICE

IX

The Teleplay Outline

It is customary to submit an outline (or synopsis) of the writer's teleplay together with the manuscript itself. The restrictions on their time make it usually impossible, always difficult, for the producer or his story editor to read through an entire teleplay of whose origin or quality they know nothing. These people desire, sometimes demand, a resumé of the story told by your teleplay which they can read quickly. If the outline's effect is to make the teleplay sound like an interesting possibility, then the producer or editor will read the full material (which it is advisable to submit with the outline rather than to hold in reserve awaiting an expression of interest).

The writer who lives at a distance from his market, who is mailing his teleplay from Richmond, Indiana, or Montpelier, Idaho, will find it imperative to include an outline with his full material. So will the writer who lives only a telephone call away from the studio, since the basic reason applies to each.

Because the preliminary decision on your submission will be made on the basis of your outline, you can see how vital it is to learn how to construct a good one.

Putting your story into outline form is an art in itself. The kind of outline I am talking about must be expertly written because it is designed to stimulate the producer's interest in your submission. It bears little resemblance to the grab-bag of ideas, character sketches, snatches of dialogue, and plot possibilities you have put down for your own use as a worksheet in composing your teleplay.

The outline now under discussion—the "selling synopsis" in the old-fashioned phrase current in movie story departments—must be smartly tailored. It should be clear, interesting, and brief: a faithful reflection in miniature of your teleplay. There are certain things that will help in writing your outline, but before we go into them I want to underline the importance of submitting a complete teleplay along with your outline when you first attempt to break into television.

Submitting an outline alone is not enough for the writer who has yet to sell his first teleplay.

The reason is obvious. As a writer of teleplays you are an unknown quantity to the producer and his story editor. They may like your story very much, but if they have only a brief outline to go on, lacking the fully developed teleplay that shows them you can write good dialogue and manipulate your plot elements professionally, they will very probably offer to buy the story outline for substantially less than you would receive for a complete teleplay, proposing to turn it over to an experienced writer, known to them, for development into a shooting script. If you refuse to take the time and trouble to write a detailed script, you can lose as much as two thousand dollars. More important, as regards your career, you will deny yourself the vital *solo* writing credit which can open so many doors to you. Producers are impressed by the credit on the screen, "Written by Edgar A. Melville." But the credit putting Mr. Melville in second place that reads "Teleplay by Jane Fenimore, Story by Edgar A. Melville," is unlikely to create a demand for the Melville services.

Once you are an old hand (and one successful script turns you into a known quantity) you will not have to invest so much time in an uncertain project. An established writer can submit a brief outline (it is even accepted practice to tell a story to a producer instead of submitting it in writing) and his ability to develop it is taken on faith. It might, of course, be rejected for one of several reasons: because the subject was taboo for the program's sponsor, or because the producer was already working on a story with a similar theme. If he is turned down, the writer has not spent inordinate time on his submission. If it is accepted, he is then assigned to expand it into shape for production, and he writes his teleplay with the assurance that he will be paid for it.

As a novice, you should submit an outline, too, but if producer interest is whetted, then be prepared with a television script. It is the proof that you are competent to adapt your story idea to its final pattern.

To be both dogmatic and repetitious: *it is essential that the unknown writer's first story for television be submitted in complete teleplay form.*

I have worked on both sides of the fence. I have sold stories and bought them. And as a producer I have rejected outlines, and as a writer I have had mine rejected, under the precise circumstances we are considering.

Two Examples

When *Maverick* was in its third year on the air, an unknown who worked for an aircraft company in Seattle submitted an eight-page outline for the show, a story with an amusing premise well worked out entitled *A Tale of Three Cities.* As producer, I had never heard of Robert Wright and neither had anyone else at the studio. The predictable happened. We bought the story, I assigned a seasoned writer to do the teleplay, and Wright received only story payment and secondary credit. His own story had a happy ending (at least he moved to Hollywood and became a prolific writer for television) for his next submission was in teleplay form and duly appeared on *Maverick* as *The Cruise of the Cynthia B.* It might just as well have happened with *Three Cities.*

A young woman named Mae Malotte, who had never written a line of dramatic dialogue in her life, watched *Maverick* every Sunday night for two years and got to know its characters and flavor as thoroughly as did its star, James Garner. She made use of this saturation, and wrote a strange and haunting story which told how Maverick journeyed into the Great Smokies and met a girl popularly supposed to be a witch who, in the fantastic denouement, turned out to be exactly that. The sixty-page teleplay submitted by the author, along with the usual outline, possessed dialogue and color and characterization of an extremely high order. *The Witch of Hound Dog* clearly deserved a place in the *Maverick* canon. But Miss Malotte's outline by itself did not, in its ten pages, demonstrate that mastery of teleplay elements which caused the script to be purchased. It told the story and it made me want to read the complete material, which is what a good outline should do. But the plot by itself—if there had not been a teleplay to show its detailed treatment—would probably have struck me as too weird and far-fetched for the show. For one thing, humor was a strong feature of the teleplay. There was not much of it in the outline. Humor is difficult to put across when you are squeezing your story into ten pages or less. The outline would have been rejected. The teleplay was purchased because it demonstrated what an outline could not.

The television producer is more inclined to be afraid of the unknown than are other men. He works under constant pressure, he is held accountable for the spending of large sums, and he is not going to run the risk of making a costly mistake by deliberately involving himself with an unknown quantity. A well-written teleplay is the new writer's insurance against being consigned to that category.

But do not get the impression that it is unnecessary to bother with an outline for your first submission. It is a convenience for the producer. As we noted at the start of this chapter, it enables him to form a preliminary opinion of your story's suitability for his show. But it can be of mutual benefit. The outline may stimulate the producer to read your teleplay then and there, having received a favorable first impression of your story. Without the outline, your teleplay may be tossed into the pile of story submissions on the producer's desk, to be read "when he has time." And the time may not come until he has bought his quota of stories for the season and is no longer in the market.

Brief, Clear, Interesting

A good outline is more than a short version of a long story. It must be several things if it is to rouse interest in the prospective buyer. It must be clear, of course, and easy to read. And the first rule for clarity is not to introduce so many characters at the beginning that the reader has to backtrack when he reaches page three because he has become confused about who is who and must reread page one to find out.

Do not overcompress the plot elements. You have a limited amount of space, and it is wise to omit unimportant features of the plot and concentrate on the main story line. (Speaking of space, the outline for an hour teleplay should be about ten pages long. This is short enough to be read in a few minutes, long enough to present a little of the color and flavor that characterize the teleplay. Outlines are conventionally in the present tense. And they should be double-spaced for easy reading.) It is a mistake to think you can include in the outline everything from the orginal script. If you do try to give equal space to every step, the outline will not only be difficult to follow but there will not be enough emphasis on key dramatic moments (crises) and your story will seem rather flat. So never hesitate to omit minor characters, whose inclusion can impede the story's drive, or scenes not vital to the plot.

Do hit the high spots. Select three or four scenes each of which is a crisis. The last one should be the climax. Describe them in some detail. Dramatize them. By this I do not mean going suddenly into screenplay form. Borrow something of the short story technique: let the scenes play out fully, get some vividness into your description, and use a line or two of significant dialogue to bring the scene to life and thrust home its dramatic force. But use no more than eight or nine short dialogue excerpts throughout. Carefully selected, they will enhance your characters and give the synopsis dimension and vitality.

The outline passages linking these scenes should be sparse and lean, devised to present information clearly and concisely. For instance:

> In the course of that afternoon's investigation, Maynard goes to the nightwatchman's dingy little cottage and briefly interviews him. Obviously uneasy, the nightwatchman at first evades Maynard's questions, but eventually reveals that his daughter, Janet, is working as a hat check girl at the Club Orientale. Maynard hails a cab and sets out for the address.

Assume that the following scene, the meeting between Maynard and Janet, is one of your important conflict points. You highlight it with extra detail. It might start like this:

> It is a slack time at the Club, hours too early for cocktails, and Maynard finds the hat check girl idly manicuring her nails in her cubicle. Janet displays only the mildest interest when Maynard flashes his badge and questions her about the General. Of course she knows the General, says Janet, blinking artificial lashes. The General has come into the Club several times a week for, oh, simply ages.
> "Does he come in alone?"
> "Not always."
> "Who's with him?"
> Janet smiles tantalizingly. Then, savoring her words:
> "The girl you're looking for. The one you're not going to find. Because she's dead."

And so on, to the conclusion of the particular episode.

One scene in your outline that should usually be spelled out for the reader is the very beginning. Take time to describe your characters as they appear, and remember that sometimes one line of dialogue can give the essence of a personality better than a paragraph of photographic detail. Establish your setting vividly, whether it is a gloomy Appalachian glen, a bustling noisy newspaper office, or a glamorous Miami boudoir. These opening paragraphs orient your reader. He must know where he is and whom he's meeting. And he must be sufficiently interested to continue reading.

Into the Tunnel Again

I suggest that you now go back to the end of Chapter II (Part One) and examine the outline of *Tunnel of Fear,* keeping in mind what you have just been told.

It is clear, I hope, and certainly written in the present tense. It does not include everything that was seen on the television tube. Several minor figures, a conductor, a doctor, passengers on the train, are not mentioned. In the teleplay there was a brief epilogue with the conductor and some of the others entering the compartment and finding Sir Henry's body. I chose to drop this from the outline and to end at the high spot when Jerry realizes that his old partner is dead. Incidentally, my summary was much shorter than ten pages because *Tunnel* was a half-hour teleplay.

The beginning is extremely detailed as Sir Henry is carried aboard the train and Jerry watches, then scrambles into the carriage as the train starts to move. It includes almost everything to be found in the teleplay itself (for brevity, it does not reproduce the expository dialogue that reveals Sir Henry's identity and condition, but the content of that dialogue is made known).

After two sentences which summarize two pages of teleplay—

> Ignoring Sir Henry's protests, the stranger chatters away with offensive familiarity. He knows about Sir Henry, referring to him scoffingly as one of the wealthiest and most respected men in all England.

—I reached a crisis point and wrote with much more detail, carefully paraphrasing the original teleplay and using dialogue to bring out the scene's values:

```
Menacingly, the stranger asks Sir Henry if he doesn't re-
member him. They used to be good friends. Sir Henry denies
ever having seen him before. "It's been twenty years,
Henry," says the stranger, "and I've changed. But you'll
remember the name: Jerry Morgan."
```

Do not hesitate to alter, condense, or even invent lines. A faithful quotation from the teleplay may be too long for the outline. Paraphrasing the dialogue so that it conveys the feeling or spirit of the original, without quoting it in full, is often advisable.

A final thing to keep in mind about your outline writing: it is perfectly permissible to go from the subjective to the objective in your narrative style. Just don't do it too often. Switch to the objective only to present a happening more briefly and to better advantage than you could if you refrained from detaching yourself for a moment and stepping outside the frame of the story. There are several such objective spots in the *Tunnel of Fear* outline:

From a brief conversation . . . <u>we learn</u> that Sir Henry is crippled by arthritis.

<u>We know</u> by his expression that he does recognize Jerry Morgan.

The last thing <u>we see</u> before the blackness of the tunnel <u>engulfs the screen is a close-up</u> of Sir Henry's horrified face.

How to Watch Television

All writers must know their markets. You learn about yours by watching television. Instruction in this pursuit may seem unnecessary, but there are a few suggestions at this jumping-off period of your career that can be of help. Establishing sensible patterns of viewing will save you a lot of time.

Don't be too conscientious and try to watch all the story programs on the air. Six hours a week is about all the time you should spend in front of the tube if you are going to get on with your writing. You are probably familiar with most of the shows in the field of drama and comedy. If not, a look at one of the magazines that catalogue air fare should turn up four or five market possibilities. Watch these programs, settle on the one which appeals to you most, and make the decision to write for it. It is extremely important for the new television writer to channel his attention and his energies. Don't be stampeded by the flood of programs which you may hear are open for submissions and force yourself into writing for a show whose content you don't much care for simply because it allegedly represents a market.

If there are any anthology programs on the air when you read this, I suggest you consider one as your target. Since they have no continuing characters but present a different story each week and generally use a variety of subject matter, they offer the writer greater freedom than series or serials. Anthologies have alternately surged and dwindled since the great early days of *Climax!* and the first *Playhouse 90*. In their present, more robust form they are, of course, the features made for television, the Movies of the Week, the World Premieres, and the two-hour TV specials. The need for expanded subject matter in this area is enormous, and the rewards, challenges, and demands for the writer are equally great.

But a different type of program may have an affinity for you. Say you like a certain series with the same characters featured each week. You are sympathetic with them and you know something about the subject which involves them: medicine, the law, military life, teaching, or merely the lighter side of small town domesticity. If such is the case, by all means write a script for the show.

More than one student has confided to me his dissatisfaction at the prospect of working with someone else's characters instead of with his own. He wants all the work to be his: writing for a series created by another writer is thought to be hack work. This is an ego barrier. Insisting that it is an obstacle is self-indulgence, and also impractical considering the popularity of series.

Tell yourself that part of your work has been done for you. Major characters are already in existence, and if you find them interesting you are measurably ahead of the game. You can concentrate on confronting the established people with events involving other people who are your own creation. You hardly need to hear that if you don't like the characters you should stay away from that show.

Before we leave the subject of series writing, here are one or two additional pieces of counseling. Watch carefully at least three episodes of the program you have elected. Keep in mind certain things that you wouldn't bother to notice if you were merely entertaining yourself. Know the *full* names of the continuing characters. Be on the lookout for personality traits that distinguish them: explosive temper, sharp wit, homely philosophy, nervous twitches, pregnant silences, and the like. Try to get the "feel" of the show.

Does the leading character always emerge victorious in time for the last commercial or does he, like the hero of *Slattery's People,* occasionally lose out in the interests of credibility? Do the stories abound in action? Is there always a physical climax—a chase, a fight, or somebody on a high ledge threatening to jump? Is it an adult program hospitable to a thought-provoking idea once in a while? Or is its plot always focused on such things as the identity of the man with the limp who is pretending to be a Scotland Yard inspector? Are there certain turns of phrase characteristic of the leading lady? (The heroine of the old *Mr. and Mrs. North* series had the irritating habit of exclaiming "Gollies!" with little or no provocation.)

It is well to scribble notes on such matters during the breaks for commercials. You will soon have a dossier of your chosen program, indispensable when you write your teleplay.

X

The Buyers and the Sellers

"Will I need an agent?"

This is one of the urgent questions a student writer asks when the teleplay he has written and rewritten and polished seems to him to have a chance of being accepted for production.

The answer is yes. And the more successful you become, the more you will need one.

A second question, perhaps more pertinent at this point, is how you go about getting one.

We may begin by understanding the functions of a writer's agent (or artist's manager, to give him his formal title). The agent is supposed to represent the writer and his work in the business negotiations connected with the sale of his writing. The widespread view that all an agent does is sell your story for a good price, and deduct ten per cent for his pains, is too simple a definition. It rouses the suspicion (also widely held) that a writer, having sold some scripts and thereby having made something of a name for himself in television production circles, does not need an agent. Why not keep all the money instead of paying a substantial amount for an unnecessary service?

Here's the trouble: the more successful a writer without an agent becomes, the more time he will be forced to devote to those business details—bargaining for a price for his story, investigating his market, discussing contracts—which take him away from writing. We have what seems a paradox, but really isn't, that an established writer who has no difficulty selling his output needs an agent more than the neophyte struggling to make his first sale.

The good agent is guide and advisor as well as salesman. The value of his guidance in the submission of your scripts is quickly summarized. He knows which television programs are open for story submissions; he knows which ones will make their debuts soon and are presently searching for story material; he knows in general the types of stories likely to find favor with active producers. It is his job to be in touch, and keep you in touch, with the markets you must reach.

Over and beyond the immediate story sale, the kind of agent you should have can also help guide your career. He can steer you along a certain course to successful writing that you might not have had the acumen to take on your own. He can prevent you from making mistakes. The shrewd agent regards his client as a long-term investment, and he will on occasion take the credit and let the cash go if, in his judgment, the credit promises greater rewards.

The Long View

If this sounds extravagant, consider the history of a woman I shall call Jean Roxburgh who earned a modest living writing television scripts for some fifteen years. Suddenly she hit the jackpot: she was offered a long-term assignment at a very high figure. She had written several teleplays for a network program which attracted mass audiences by presenting soap opera plots in an elaborate nineteenth century western setting. Network executives, pleased with Jean's skill in mastering the show's dubious formula (dubious artistically, at any rate), proposed that she work exclusively for the program for two years. She would receive more money during this period than she had earned in the preceding ten years. As a further inducement, the network's legal department worked out an intricate schedule of tax benefits for her.

Nevertheless, Jean's agent persuaded her to refuse the tempting bait. He was not dazzled by the sum. He argued that if his client signed the contract, she would be out of circulation for two years, unable to accept television or feature assignments of greater prestige. Two years of association with this soap-and-saddle saga would type her as a hack writer. Consequently, when the two-year stint was up, she would find it difficult to sell her writing services to programs of superior calibre.

Instead of certain money and security, Jean, continuing to free-lance, got several television writing assignments, carefully selected by her agent, on shows of greater distinction. The work enhanced her reputation and led to a contract with a major studio to write the screenplay for an important feature film. . . .

A good agent is a critic and an editor and a planner. Jean's agent assessed her possibilities as a writer and saw that they would not be realized unless her career took a different direction. If, on the other hand, he had concluded that her talent was limited he would have arranged for her to sign that network contract the instant it was offered. He reasoned that over a period of years Jean would make more money if she did not sign. The agent nurtures a writer's career only as a means to an end. His ultimate concern is with how much money he can make out of his clients. And this is a most excellent thing for you, because he can't make money unless you make money.

All agents are not as farsighted as Jean's, but practically all of them excel at bargaining for the maximum payment for your story. They are thoroughly familiar with prices paid for stories, they know very well what the traffic will bear, and they earn their commissions by usually getting you more than you would have asked yourself. Also—and this is important—the agent insures that the relationship between you and your producer is restricted to the work at hand, the actual writing of the script. The agent does your haggling for you, and if the producer thinks your demands are outrageous he blames the agent. The agent is a very handy fellow to have around as a middle man and buffer.

The Hurdle Again

Since agents are not in business for their health, they tend to be fully as cautious when they are approached by an unknown writer as are producers.

We have just looked at some of the things an agent does for his writer clients. It follows that the average successful agent, with a string of these clients, is too busy to spend time trying to further the interests of a writer who has not yet proved anything. Many are too busy even to read a script by a yet unproduced writer unless someone whose opinion they respect calls it to their attention. Nothing creates such a favorable impression on an agent as the knowledge that somebody else has been favorably impressed. It is a rare agent who will trouble with a submission that arrives in his office cold, unannounced, and unrecommended.

There is no sense in blaming agents for this state of affairs. Keeping the door open for writers they never heard of, on the outside chance that the unknown may have talent instead of being one of those ambitious incompetents who abound in Hollywood, is simply not their business. They are not running schools, and they are the operators of talent agencies, not employment agencies. They undertake to sell stories, and the talents of the men and women who write the stories, because they believe both stories and talents have commercial value. It is futile to argue that they should also be the discoverers of new talent. Despite this, many agents pride themselves on helping new writers, pushing them on to fame and fortune. *But the new writer has first to do something that will evoke the agent's attention.*

It all boils down to this: you will spend as much time and energy establishing a connection with an agent as you will in selling a story. If you work hard enough you will almost certainly prevail on an agent to read your script and, if it is good, to undertake to sell it. You will need persistence, industry, patience, and the heart to be undiscouraged by refusals. These qualities of course are what you need to sell the story for yourself. And the sale of a story is the "something" that will evoke the agent's attention.

After your first sale, look around for an agent. Make your selection carefully. You want somebody to handle your work who has those attributes of guide, critic, editor, super-salesman, and prophet that we have been hymning. You should pick up some leads pointing to this paragon from the people you meet at studio or network when you are trying to sell your first story. Other writers are the best source of information about agents because they tend to be highly critical of their agents, and if you hear one praise his agent, that agent will be worth investigating.

Indemnifying the Producer

In submitting your story yourself, go through accepted channels. But augment the conventional approach with whatever ingenuity and common sense you possess. If you are in a position to do so, take advantage of any acquaintances who are connected with the show. If you know a minor actor, a cutter, a stand-in, an assistant director, or a script clerk, talk to him about your story and see if he is willing to mention it to somebody in authority who can influence its purchase. No stigma attaches to the use of private influence in a business society which only shrugs at nepotism. If you possess any strings, pull them.

But you will also submit your script in the orthodox fashion. Most story departments will accept scripts for consideration from new writers without agents if the writer signs a standard release form and submits it with his script. Request this form (by mail or telephone) from the program's story editor or from the office of its producer. It represents your assurance that the work you submit is original, and that you will indemnify the company for any damages they may have to pay (arising from libel or plagiarism suits) as a result of producing your script.

The origin of this precaution can be traced back to the days of silent movies. When motion picture production began to be a very profitable business, the large studios were increasingly plagued by what they called "nuisance suits." The typical nuisance suit—for plagiarism—was brought by an amateur writer who contended that Multimillion Productions had stolen the idea for their picture, *A Modern Cinderella,* from the plaintiff's scenario, *Cutglass Slippers,* submitted to the Multimillion story department long before the release of defendant's film. These suits for the most part proved to have no legal validity whatsoever, but they were troublesome and expensive to defend.

In addition to the honest but mistaken amateurs, out-and-out con men would often aim a plagiarism suit at a wealthy picture studio in the expectation that the company would settle out of court rather than tie up its overburdened legal department with a long court action. In the 1930's and 1940's most film companies refused to consider unpublished story material that did not come to them from a recognized agent, and any flat package arriving in the studio mail was instantly returned unopened to its sender on the supposition that it was a manuscript whose author was probably either larcenous or lunatic. A reputable agent routinely insures a company accepting a submission against baseless suing. When television arrived, and a season's program needed from twenty-six to fifty-two stories a year to fulfill its commitment, the demand for scripts attained such proportions that no company could afford to ignore the amateur and the beginner, whether or not he had an agent: hence, the release form which causes the sensitive writer to think he is regarded as a suspicious character. He is—but that's the accepted system. Submit to it if you want to submit your teleplay.

Waiting for Word

Another question that obsesses the writer who is trying to sell his first teleplay is: How long will it take to hear something after I submit my story? The only honest answer is that it is absolutely impossible to predict. Your script may be returned (or accepted) in a week. It may not be given a final disposition for a year. This is not hyperbole. I was once guilty, as a story editor, of keeping a writer's script for eleven months without accepting or rejecting it. It was a story I liked and wanted to see produced on our program, but the producer had reservations and for a long time I was not able to sell it to him. Then the day came when a script we had been counting on for filming on a certain date turned out disastrously, not an uncommon crisis in television. We were in acute need of something to substitute for it on the shooting stage. I was authorized to buy the story and the author's patience was finally rewarded.

Another writer I know submitted a story to *77 Sunset Strip,* a television program of a number of years ago. He put nothing on paper but told the story to the Warner Brothers story editor who made notes and committed them to an outline himself. Months passed and there was no word from Warner's. My friend assumed his story had been turned down, and since there was no manuscript to be sent back he put the matter out of his mind. He put it out of his mind so successfully that nine months later, when his agent called to announce that Warner's was buying the story and he was to start work on the teleplay immediately, he was panic-stricken because he couldn't recall how it went. He would have been lost without the notes taken by the editor. (This anecdote contributes to my distrust of verbalizing rather than committing to paper.) In this instance the writer had approached the 77 show at the time when the producer was "bought up" for that season, and the story was tabled for future reference. When the network over whose facilities the telefilms produced at the Warner studio were shown renewed *77 Sunset Strip* for another year, the search for stories was on again, and those scripts and outlines that were being held were brought out for reconsideration.

But on the other hand you may be so fortunate as to take in a script at the precise time the producer sorely needs story material for his show. If he likes the story, the speed with which you will be summoned to sign a contract and receive a check will amaze and gratify you. It will also be the source of future unhappiness if you decide that this promptness is normal procedure and expect all subsequent transactions to be as rapidly consummated.

When it comes to selling a teleplay, it is idle to look for rules by which to abide, for there are no rules. The purchase of a story for television production is governed by so many imponderables, ranging from personal whim to obscure but vital network policy, that it is best to submit your script and return to your typewriter to work on something else. This is the only known method to avoid worrying about what is happening to your creation. If you have heard nothing at the end of three weeks, I think it advisable to check by letter or telephone with the office (producer's or story editor's) which has your story. Be governed by that office's reaction as to the frequency with which you check thereafter. Your object is to keep in touch without making a pest of yourself.

A Curious Profession

The story editor, as you will have gathered, is a person very important to you. Although only in rare instances will he have the authority to buy your story without consulting his producer, his word carries great weight. Another reason why you should know something about this key figure is that you may find yourself in his job some day if you make a career of film and television writing. Few men and women today are story editors without being writers too. The duties of a television story editor, and his creative function, are enormously greater than those of his direct ancestor, the old-time movie story editor. He does far more with much less.

When Hollywood was the world leader in the production of feature films, and television's competition loomed on the horizon as a cloud no bigger than a B picture, the story editor headed a large department of readers and sub-editors. He had a literary background (usually), but he was not primarily a writer. It was his function to read screenplays, movie treatments, and advance copies of published books, most of this story material having been condensed to synopsis form by his staff of readers or, as they prefer to be known, story analysts. The story editor recommended to studio producers such stories and plays as he felt could be turned into good movies. If the producer agreed, and the head of the studio approved, the editor then negotiated with the author or his agent for the purchase of the property. The editor earned his salary because his background and experience enabled him to size up a story's potentialities. When applied to a book not yet published, the editor's skill in predicting its reception by the reading public, and his shrewdness in buying it for a reasonable price, were qualities esteemed by the story editor's studio. Nobody, as yet, expected him to be a writer, too.

When *Gone With the Wind* was just a tall stack of galley proofs and nobody, including the author Margaret Mitchell and her agent, dreamed of the impact it would have on the public, David Selznick's sharp-eyed story editor was able to buy the motion picture rights for fifty thousand dollars, a preposterously low sum for a book which in a few months would head the best seller list, stay there for years to make publishing history, and eventually be translated into a movie that would gross more money than any picture before (with the possible exception of that other epic about the Civil War, *The Birth of a Nation,* whose doubtless astronomical profits have never been accurately reckoned because of incomplete records).

Occasionally, the elaborate story department system of the movies' heyday, with its story editor, associate story editors, assistant story editors, and large staff of synopsis writers, proved embarrassingly cumbersome. One leading production company was caught napping in the case of *Gone With the Wind.* No editor or producer displayed the slightest interest in the book. This was not really strange because all they knew about it was contained in a twenty-page synopsis written by a story analyst who, for reasons still mysterious, outlined the first half of the novel in nineteen pages and gave exactly one page to the dramatic series of events involving Scarlett O'Hara and Rhett Butler that took place after the Civil War.

The transition in the late 1940's and early 1950's from the movies' method of finding stories to television's drastically different streamlined operation was painful. The early television companies made the mistake of trying to do what the picture companies did but with very little money to spend. What resulted was the one-man story department, a depressing, short-lived institution. The procedure, in those days of *My Favorite Story, Playhouse of Stars, Fireside Theater,* and other forgotten half hours, was to engage a studio sub-editor or reader to read story submissions, write synopses, comb the libraries for adaptable short stories, bargain for stories, engage writers and help them with their stories, and draw up contracts for their services. Under these conditions some story editors resigned and went into a sane line of work. Those with talent and stamina remained and developed into the story supervisor of today, often a combination of writer, story editor, and producer. His life may be just as harassed as it was, but his efforts at least are more efficiently applied.

Variations

Not every person whose main concern is with television story material has the same title or the same duties. Some are staff writers as well as editors, and some are producers or associate producers. The story head in many cases has originated the program on which he works, in which case he will be accorded a separate credit card among the screen titles reading "Created by John Parker" in addition to the credit that describes his active and continuing function on the show.

In unusual and conspicuous instances, like *Twilight Zone,* Rod Serling's series, a program may have virtually a single authority, with the show's creator exercising control as producer, supervisor of the scripts, and author of many of its teleplays. The advantage of this program structure to the contributing writer from outside is his privilege of dealing with one person, in a position to buy or reject his story, instead of a veritable committee. Too often, the writer who seems to be negotiating with a story editor is actually waiting for the approval of the editor's superiors who can include a producer, an associate producer, a network executive, the sponsor's advertising agency, and possibly even the star of the show, if the star's contract accords him story approval.

But since both the solo command and the hierarchy of story

approvers are extremes, it is probable that you will submit your story to an editor whose characteristics run along the following line:

He is a writer with ten or more produced teleplays to his credit. He may have written a few feature screenplays. His contract calls for him to write six of the show's segments himself. He has very solid notions about the kind of story he (and/or the producer) wants for the show, strong likes and dislikes. He frequently has ideas for stories which, since he lacks time to telescript them himself, he turns over to other writers for development into teleplays.

He suggests subjects for stories: if your first submission is favorably received, he will outline for you the kind of story he is looking for, one, for example, with a strong love interest, or a tour de force which has only one character besides the hero, or a detective mystery to provide a change of pace in the series.

The story editor must take care how he presents these suggestions to the writers. He is not permitted to order or advise you to turn out a certain kind of story on the mere chance that it will find favor, because this would be a serious violation of a cardinal Writers Guild rule designed to prevent what is ambiguously called "speculative writing." The phrase is ambiguous because all writing that is not contracted for is literally speculative. In the sense the Guild uses the term, speculative writing refers to any writing which a production executive requests a writer to do for him without agreeing to pay the writer for it. The editor or producer may say to you, "We'd like to find a good story about a missionary to the Indians." He may *not* say, "Give me two or three pages on the missionary-Indian idea and I'll see if the sponsor goes for it." It is entirely up to you whether you invest time and talent in constructing a story of the kind you hear described. It would be naive to assume that the rule about speculative writing is never broken, especially in instances where writer and editor have a rapport and the editor feels reasonably certain that a sale will result if his advice is followed; but a strong reason for violations not being widespread is that the story editor, as well as the writer, is a member of the Writers Guild.

If you are not a member of the Guild at the time you submit your first teleplay, you will be soon after you make your first sale. We'll hear more about the Guild and its workings in the next chapter.

Working under Duress

Of the television story editors I know approximately seventy-five per cent are, first and importantly, television *writers*. Writing is their continuing profession although at one period they may be working as editors and at another their names may appear in the television screen credits as associate producers. This year they are occupying salaried posts, directing the work of other writers as well as contributing stories and teleplays of their own as part of their contractual obligations. Next season some of them, in all probability, will be free-lance writers again.

The other twenty-five per cent have differing backgrounds. One is the literary editor for a metropolitan newspaper. He does no writing for the television program which engages him, but suggests story ideas, uncovers sources of story material, and develops (for television) new writers with whom his book reviewing has put him in touch. Two others entered television after years as associate story editors at two major studios in Hollywood, and before that were movie story analysts or readers. One is a former New York publishing house executive, and one came into television by creating and producing his own program in the early 1960's. Finally, the story editor and head writer for a popular program is a former actor. He alternated between playing in television pictures and writing them before he decided to concentrate exclusively on the latter. (The actor-writer combination in the theater is a tradition that extends quite a few centuries into the past. Sophocles was a member of the chorus, on occasion, in the Greek drama. Shakespeare acted, as did Ben Jonson and Molière. In our time Harold Pinter was an actor in England for seven years before he wrote his first play in 1957.)

If all the story editors, regardless of how their personalities may differ, have in common certain nervous character quirks, the reason is not hard to find. Many years ago the television critic of a national magazine emphasized the constant pressure that bore down on the creative workers in the young medium, and observed that nobody should get himself involved in the production of a television program who did not enjoy the unrelenting sense of impending disaster. Few people are so inextricably involved in television production as the story editor, and the passage of years has done nothing to dispel the preoccupation with disaster.

Let me give you a look at one hour in the day of a story editor, taking care to assure you first that the description is neither untypical nor exaggerated.

We will suppose that this is an hour early in the morning and that your teleplay and outline have been placed on his desk.

He starts to read the outline. After three sentences the telephone rings. It is the show's producer, demanding drastic revisions in the third act of *Behind the Lines* which must go before the cameras Monday morning if the picture is to be ready for showing on its scheduled air date. The editor picks up his other phone, locates the writer, and engages in a three-way story conference which everyone hopes will result in the writer doing over the third act, with some visual drama substituted for the present static dialogue scenes, and delivering the changes to the studio no later than the following afternoon.

The story editor hangs up, returns to your outline and gets halfway through the first page before his office door opens and the man from the advertising agency, who represents the program's sponsor, enters with an expression that says he has a problem. He announces that the sponsor has experienced grave doubts about the story outline he approved two weeks ago and which the editor, on the strength of the approval, has purchased and assigned to be written as a teleplay. The sponsor, who manufactures automobiles, has been advised by an aide that it might be embarrassing to have the sponsor name on a picture which opens with a head-on collision between two automobiles. The editor, after unhappily pointing out that the auto wreck is the story's pivotal situation, promises to have it changed to a train wreck and makes a note to break the news to the writer and also to check with the film library to see if stock footage of a railroad accident is available.

As the agency man exits, mollified, the editor's secretary sticks her head in the door to remind him that this afternoon is the deadline for composing that memorandum to the producer analyzing the possibilities of adapting a current novel into a two-part script for the program. As an afterthought, she mentions the presence in the outer office of two important writers who appeared promptly for their appointment with the editor twenty minutes ago and are becoming restive. As the two writers come crowding in, the editor's phones start ringing in unison, and our hour is up. Suspecting that from here on in things will get increasingly out of hand, the editor picks up your script and outline and stuffs them in his briefcase, to be taken home and read in comparative peace, probably over the weekend. And this is the best break you could possibly have: if he persisted in trying to read your script under *these* circumstances, he would inevitably end up disliking it.

This is a glimpse into the real world of television. This is the arena in which you will battle for your bread and butter. If you can see it as exciting instead of terrifying, a challenge rather than a nightmare, and electrifying as well as shocking, then you probably have the requisite gladiatorial temperament. There will be people on your side to counsel and assist. Those people are the subject of the next chapter.

XI

WGAw

The initials of the chapter title stand for Writers Guild of America, West. All television writers based in Hollywood belong to it. Its headquarters are in Los Angeles where it functions as the union for West Coast television, motion picture, and radio writers. Its activities are many, but its primary purpose is to represent writers in collective bargaining. The WGA has two branches; the other one—WGAe—is located in New York.

Not all writers belong to the Guild. Novelists, historians and other writers of prose, as well as playwrights whose output is exclusively for the theater, are regarded as independent contractors by the Federal Government under the terms of the Taft-Hartley Act. They are in business for themselves. WGA members—the television and screen and radio writers—are considered employees engaged by the studios, production companies, and networks to whom they sell stories and from whom they get their writing assignments. Novelists and short story writers can't strike. Writers eligible for Guild membership can.

You do not have to be a member of the Guild (indeed you cannot) to offer your first script for sale. But if it is bought you must apply for Guild membership in the television branch within thirty days of purchase. This makes the Guild sound like a closed shop. Actually it is not, because in the contract between the Guild and the producers (which is called the Minimum Basic Agreement, the MBA) the Guild agrees to admit to membership anyone hired by a company to write for television. The acceptance for production of one teleplay (or a story outline with or without an assignment to develop it into teleplay form) entitles you to associate membership in the Writers Guild.

As an associate member you have all the rights (including protection in your dealings with producers) of full, or active, membership except the rights to vote, hold office, and serve on committees. The writer is admitted to active membership when he receives more credits (a credit is your name on the screen). You need eighteen points under the Guild's unit system to qualify for active membership. A credit as sole writer of an hour teleplay gives you six points; you receive three points for a half-hour television credit. But you can become a full member in the screen writers' branch by getting one individual credit as the author of a theatrical feature; a movie credit counts for eighteen points. There are similar requirements for active membership in the radio wing.

Approximately 3,000 writers belong to the Guild in Los Angeles. About 2,500 write for television (or at least hold membership in that branch). Some of these are also screen writers. The initiation fee is $200. Dues are $10 a quarter plus one and a quarter per cent of all your earnings as a writer for any of the mediums involved. Like other guilds and unions, WGA has a pension plan, group insurance, and a credit union. It performs many professional tasks and engages in a number of professional-social activities. A vital service is the collection of writers' royalty payments for reruns. Another is the registration of unsold story material, for a nominal fee, as a form of copyright protection. This service is also available to writers who are not Guild members. The Guild checks each individual contract made between a writer and a producer to insure that it conforms to the Minimum Basic Agreement in all details.

An Eventful History

The Guild was originally the SWG, the Screen Writers Guild. It was in existence for five years before it was recognized by the producers of Hollywood. The organization of movie writers was part of the great drive for unionization of all crafts that went on in the picture industry in the late 1930's.

No craft needed a union more. In 1936 there were a few "name" writers who commanded salaries comparable to those paid stars and producers. But the mass of movie writers were underpaid and victimized. Their employment could be terminated without notice, they were frequently tricked into speculative writing by the promise of assignments that never materialized, and they had their story ideas stolen. Their names appeared on the screen in smaller type than those of directors and producers. They were workers without dignity in a milieu where status determined income. Their fight for collective bargaining rights was bitterly resisted over a five-year period by the producers. The National Labor Relations Board, charging that the studios had joined in a conspiracy to smash the Guild, certified the SWG as the legal collective bargaining agency for movie writers in 1938, but it was three years before the producers surrendered and agreed to negotiate.

We lack the space to detail the Guild's stormy history. It is hard to find a placid period of more than a year or two in the last quarter of a century. When the Guild wasn't battling the producers, the membership was fighting among themselves, throwing out the Communists who tried to run things, and then crusading against McCarthyism. But always the fight to improve the terms under which the writer worked went on: by 1953, when television and radio writers were included in the Guild, the working conditions of the Hollywood writer had improved perceptibly. And, for the most part, they have continued to improve. Occasionally, the ultimate weapon—the strike—has been used, not always successfully.

The name change—to the WGA—came with the admission of the writers from television and radio. Talks with a view to their inclusion had gone on for several years prior to 1953 in an atmosphere of acrimonious confusion. Many writers didn't want to join the Guild, independent unions were set up only to be aborted, jurisdictional disputes broke out, and negotiations over the merger collapsed several times before common interests were recognized by the majority.

The confusion stemmed from identification of television with radio rather than with motion pictures. The new medium of entertainment came into the home like radio, it was broadcast by the networks like radio, and the big shows originated in New York instead of on the West Coast. It was several years before the steady advance of filmed television, produced in the same studios where "regular" movies were shot, impressed those concerned with the new orientation towards motion pictures. A strong cultural resistance, too, was involved. The best work in television was being done by New York writers, and the quality of Coast-written shows was generally bad. The men responsible for the admired anthology plays of the East opposed membership in a movie union whose writers they considered inferior. But a good writer, like a bad one, has only a single vote. The opponents of the merger were outnumbered, and the Writers Guild of America, an expansion of rather than a successor to the Screen Writers Guild, was voted into existence.

What You'll Be Paid

The television writer, several contracts and four strikes later, is considerably better off than he was in 1953. In the first writer-producer MBA, the Guild secured a minimum of $700 to be paid the writer of a half-hour story and teleplay, with proportionate fees for longer scripts. Since then the terms have been bettered several times. The current minimum for the same work (a half-hour teleplay from the writer's own story, not an adaptation of someone else's original) is $2,225. You cannot be paid *less* than the established minimum. If the producer buys your story outline only (and assigns another writer to the teleplay) the half-hour program figure is only $809.00. Remember what you read in Chapter IX: the new writer should have a full teleplay to back up the story outline he submits.

The minimum payment for an hour-length script (story and teleplay) is $3,678; for a ninety-minute program, $5,332. The MBA includes provisions for all possible contingencies: the sums that must be paid for rewrites and dialogue polishes, for instance, and the financial arrangement the producer makes if he cuts off the writer after the first draft teleplay and engages a second writer to work on the script. If you wish to go further into the basic contract stipulations, you may obtain information from the Guild offices. Writers Guild of America, West is located at 8955 Beverly Boulevard, Los Angeles, California 90048. The address of Writers Guild of America, East is 1212 Avenue of the Americas, New York, New York 10036.

Can a new writer making his first sale hope to get more than minimum compensation? Surprisingly, yes. Few producers pay as little as the MBA figures. The producer has a story costs budget, carefully worked out in relation to his over-all production expenses. The amount to be paid for a script should not be set too low. If it is, the producer is going to attract only unknown writers and those with records of bad or mediocre work who cannot get assignments elsewhere.

On an average half-hour show the maximum amount for a teleplay is usually about $3,500. This does not mean that the producer never goes above or below that figure; it means that at the end of the production season, during which he made thirteen, or twenty-six, or thirty-nine pictures, his financial statement should show that his average story costs per picture did not exceed $3,500. For a good teleplay from a well-known writer he will pay $4,500, compensating for the overpayment by buying stories from other writers who are not in such favorable bargaining positions for somehat lower figures. The need to balance the story budget helps to explain why a novice can frequently sell a script to a program which also uses big name writers.

You can realistically expect to get $2,500, perhaps more, from the sale of your first half-hour script to television; for an hour show, somewhere between $4,000 and $4,500. There is no guarantee, unfortunately, that you won't run into a penny-pincher who will try to get your teleplay for the legal minimum. But neither is there any assurance that some unscrupulous type won't suggest that you do some speculative writing with no arrangement for payment. There are hazards. Keep your eyes open.

A program's success or failure, as indicated by the controversial Nielsen rating system, has little to do with prices paid for stories. (It obviously does have something to do with the number of scripts bought.) A budget is set up long before a program makes its debut on the air. Estimates of story costs are established in an atmosphere of optimism and high hope. Months later, when the new show is being murdered by its competition and the network is ready to chop it off, the money for story purchases is the same as when the show's sponsors anticipated a long run. Annihilation, not retrenchment, is the only solution in this electronic wonder world. A writer-student in my workshop, Dorothy Gravage, sold her first teleplay to a half-hour program, *Kentucky Jones,* two weeks after the announcement that it would go permanently off the air at the season's finish. She received the going rate for her script, one of several needed to complete the producers' one-season commitment.

If the rewards for writing television are substantial, the primary reason is not pressure by agents or competition among producers. It is that minimum scale established and subsequently raised at the bargaining table by aggressive Guild representatives. Every benefit the writer receives has been fought for. If demands had not been diligently pressed, the minimum would have stayed at $700 and you would be getting perhaps $1,000 instead of $3,500 for your half-hour teleplay.

Negotiating

Since the first edition of this book appeared in 1966 the Writers Guild has won several considerable victories and repaired one major mistake. Its history in recent years, if not as fierce and stormy as was its first decade, has been lively enough to shake up even the most unflappable members of the motion picture and television industries. It has threatened to go on strike twice since 1966. These two threats evaporated at the bargaining table, but the third cry of "Wolf!" was genuine, and the Guild pulled its membership out of studios and broadcasting companies for several months in 1973 in a partly successful effort to win a catalog of demands ranging from higher minimums to control over "hyphenates"—those writers who are members of the Guild but also function as producers and management.

At various times between 1964 and 1974 the Writers Guild has engaged in acrimonious confrontation with the literary agents of Hollywood over contractual representation, with the Producers Association over better pay and conditions for writers, and with the Producers' Guild. The last named, not to be confused with the Association, which represents management and capital investment, is composed of men who are assigned to produce individual motion pictures and programs for television. Many of its members also belong to the Writers Guild, and this dual membership has given rise to a feud that has been fought and appealed in the courts at rather tiresome length. The question, of course, is who is going to exercise the more sizeable clout in the members' dealings with the film and television concentrates. Is the writer-producer essentially a writer or a producer? What is the exact position of an employee who theoretically can be hired or fired by himself? Interesting questions.

The belligerent vigilance of the Writers Guild has made its point. The policy has paid off—and so have the producers. As a result of the contract negotiations of the late 1960s and the strike of 1973 the position of the television writer (and the screen writer as well) is markedly better than it was ten years ago. And infinitely better, as we have seen, than it was in the early 1950s.

The major mistake referred to above concerns what at first seemed to be an important concession made by the television producers to the writers. The principal writer demand in the crippling strike of 1960 was for permanent participation in revenue from reruns. For seven years since 1953, television writers had received residual payments for reruns of the shows they had written, but the royalties applied only to the first five reruns, and they were limited to the United States and Canada. The percentages were satisfactory enough, but the limit to five rerun payments seemed unfair to writers who knew that a top show like *Dragnet* was shown scores of times in the domestic markets in addition to being seen all over the world for many years. The Guild was convinced that the foreign market was a gold mine from which writers had been excluded. The main demand in the 1960 strike, then, was for writer participation in all domestic and foreign rerun revenues in perpetuity. It was futile for the television producers to insist that the writers were seriously overestimating the returns from the foreign market and that Guild members would not receive as much from permanent worldwide royalties as they were getting under the old contract's residual provisions. The Guild wrote off this contention as managerial propaganda and pressed its demand.

After resisting for five months, the television producers capitulated. There followed two years of negotiations after which the writers were given what they had asked for, continuing participation in the profits from their pictures. They received 4 percent of the gross amount for which each picture they had written was sold—in all markets throughout the world.

Disillusionment came speedily. It came with the discovery that producers did not sell television programs in the foreign market for fantastic sums but for merely what they could get. And often what they could get was shockingly small. Writers accustomed to fat residual checks for reruns now received as their share payments amounting to tiny fractions of the old sums. Before the writers worked out a second settlement with the producers in 1966 I received one residual check amounting to nine cents for a rerun in Zamboanga—or was it New South Wales? In any event the nine cent royalty did not even make a topic of conversation: too many other writers had similar experiences.

The 1966 residual agreement, which proved reasonably satisfactory to all parties, was similar to an arrangement between the Producers and the Screen Actors Guild. To give you an idea of the complications in just one section of the contracts that are negotiated every few years, let me quote from the 1966 provisions for residual payments:

> For the second run not less than 50 per cent of the writer's applicable minimum salary, if the airing is on a TV network, otherwise such payment is to be not less than 40 per cent of minimum; for third run not less than 40 per cent of minimum if such a run is on a network, otherwise 30 per cent of minimum; fourth run 25 per cent of minimum; fifth run 25 per cent of minimum; sixth and all additional runs single fee of 25 per cent of minimum.

In 1970 additional benefits for both television and theatrical feature writers were obtained by the Guild after some hotly argued sessions with the producers which did not go as far as a strike. In 1973, however, leading topics of discussions included supervision over the hyphenated writer-producers and a percentage deal for writer services on cassettes to be played in the home as well as in motels and hotels. The producers put up stiff opposition, the writers threw picket lines first in front of the production companies then around the television network studios, and the second longest writers' strike was on. It concluded in the early summer of 1973 with the writers obtaining the important cassette concession and some but by no means all of their other demands.

The Problem of Credits

The Guild can loom large or small in your professional life. It is up to you. You can go to meetings, serve on committees, run for office. Not too many writers are willing to devote time to these activities. The internal enemy of the Guild is indifference. Business meetings are sparsely attended (unlike the motion picture screenings at the Guild's film society which draw crowds); and years ago it was found necessary to print RESIDUAL on the envelopes mailed containing residual checks, because members have a bad habit of tossing WGA mail into the waste basket without opening it. The attitude is: "I've paid my dues and I can't be bothered with this stuff when I have to finish the script by Thursday."

But there are enough conscientious ones to keep the group going, though not without the aid of a large and efficient paid staff. The Guild is remarkably dynamic considering that it is carried on by creative people whose temperaments and convictions are normally in conflict.

One activity, fairly well supported since it deals with a problem that can face any writer, is the work of the Arbitration Committee. Often a producer is dissatisfied with a script from a writer and assigns another writer to work on it. There have been cases where as many as four writers have worked on the same teleplay. Who gets credit for the re-rewritten script?

Suppose a producer is unhappy with a teleplay by A and gives it to B to rewrite. B changes the plot structure, adds new scenes, and rewrites the dialogue. The producer issues the final script with the writing credit reading "Written by A and B." More often than not, each writer will object to this credit and contest it. B contends that he so radically changed A's teleplay that the credit should be "Written by B." And A believes *he* is entitled to a solo writing credit because B's fiddling, he charges, did not materially alter A's original teleplay. Money and prestige are both involved in the dispute: residuals as well as credit must be shared if both writers have their names on the teleplay.

The Arbitration Committee is the machinery the Guild has devised to settle these arguments. From a panel of writers the Guild selects three to pass on each complaint. The trio of judges reads every piece of material pertaining to the case from the first story outline to the revised final teleplay. The three then determine which writer is right or whether the producer's decision to credit both should stand. Their decision is contractually binding on the producer.

A dispute may involve only two writers and still be incredibly complex. I should like to tell you about a recent arbitration because not only does it illustrate the work of the Guild committee but it depicts the kind of maddening muddle that occurs in television and into which the writer can be plunged before he knows what is happening to him. It also serves to alert the new writer to the things that can happen to him *after* he has sold his teleplay.

The history of this particular script, which wound up in arbitration, begins with a decision by the producer of an hour anthology to make a two-part film, to be shown on the program in succeeding weeks. He bought the story in outline form from a writer he knew; we shall call him Jones. The outline—it was for a spy melodrama—was twenty-five pages in length. After it was turned in (it was written after conferences between producer and writer) the studio changed its mind and decided the show should be only a one-parter. Jones wrote a second outline, simplifying and condensing his story.

Then Jones wrote a teleplay based on his second outline. The producer wanted changes so Jones made them in a revised teleplay.

After reading the second teleplay, the producer suddenly decided that Jones was incapable of writing the script the way he wanted it. Jones' employment was thereupon terminated, and the producer brought in a writer named Smith who composed a radical revision of Jones' second script. Now the madness set in that afflicts television executives when they are fearful, cruelly pressured, and unable to make up their minds.

The studio read Smith's version of the story and somebody with the power to do it decreed that the original approach should be reimplemented and the story expanded into a two-part picture. Smith went to work and wrote another teleplay twice the length of his previous one.

Now, inexplicably and without warning, Smith fell from favor. The producer hired a new writer named Brown to work on the script. Brown wrote still another teleplay which cannot be termed a rewrite, for it had a totally new theme, different locale and characters, and a dialogue style that read like Ivy Compton-Burnett's. Incidentally, Brown did not figure in the arbitration proceedings. He neither sought nor got writing credit. He finished his script, pocketed his money, and departed.

After what we must believe was due consideration, the Lord of Misrule who was producing this picture threw out the Brown script. Back came Smith, mysteriously restored to favor, and wrote what proved to be the script they shot. It was only moderately changed from his earlier teleplay that had resulted in his replacement by Brown.

The Guild's arbitration committee spent a weekend wading through this collection of teleplays and outlines and unanimously decided that the studio had been right in labeling the writing credits "Teleplay by Smith, Story by Smith and Jones." Jones had demanded the arbitration, holding that he was entitled to joint teleplay credit. But Jones had no case.

A sad and agitating story, but a guide to television writing would do the reader a disservice to conceal the fact that he will occasionally collide with abominably misdirected production procedure where there are too many fingers in the pie, where the ultimate authority lacks story sense, where incompetent hands will pick to pieces his work, and where chaos replaces efficiency.

The comparative merits of scripts submitted for arbitration are no business of the judge's. He is concerned only with how much each writer contributed to a final script, not with how good his work was. But the progress in the case we have described, through script after script, represented a dismal decline in story values.

The first outline by Jones presented a rather good story. It had some things wrong with it—situations not altogether convincing, characters not fully realized—but they could have been rectified without ripping apart the basic fabric. The philosophy that says if you keep changing something you are bound to improve it led through a labyrinth of unreasonable rewrites, wasted production time, rising story costs, and deteriorating scripts to the final teleplay judged ready for filming. It was not as good as Jones' first story.

But, as we have said, Jones had no case. Except, perhaps, a moral one . . . .

XII

An Inventory

At the conclusion of one of the television writers' workshops that I conduct, the students participate in several hours of extremely varied survey. The period is given over to questions and problems uppermost in the writers' minds. We reorient ourselves. In the process a number of ideas discovered to be out of focus become clear. Subjects, only theory when they were introduced, are reexamined in the light of usage in creative work performed as a requirement of the course. Some elements of technique are probed that were skimped in earlier sessions. One student confesses that he still tends to confuse POV SHOT and REVERSE ANGLE. Another asks for suggestions about a long silent sequence in his teleplay. Does the pantomime make the story substance clear? Is it sufficiently expressive? Still another wonders whether the frank discussion of premarital sex in his script will be acceptable to a network censor.

These sessions represent more than a review of past work. There is usually some analysis of current television programming, and out of the talk emerge practical suggestions of what it is wise to do and what one should shun.

Since this book in general parallels a workshop course, our concluding chapter reflects one of these stock-taking sessions. I have selected some topics that writers find absorbing, and others they need to be reminded of, when they reach this stage; "this stage" being the final briefing before they enter the television market as professed writers. Presumably, you are in the same position. You know something about what you're doing but not *everything*. We shall fill in a few gaps.

The Leading Character

In Chapter VII we learned something about writing characters with the actors in mind. Here is a footnote to that subject; since it concerns the approach to your teleplay, it is a good place to begin our potpourri.

A currently syndicated television series is *Bewitched.* Its running characters are a young witch, her normal husband, and her mother who is also a witch. The producer had a script whose leading figure was not a regular character but a man from outside the charmed circle. He envisioned Maurice Evans as ideal for the role. The trouble was Mr. Evans usually confined his television appearances to distinguished specials (the host for Christopher Plummer's three-hour *Hamlet*). Nevertheless, the producer sent the script to the actor who promptly agreed to play the part because he recognized that it was a good role.

The chances of selling a script are better if the story has a commanding character who stands out among the other people. The picture will be enhanced if the producer can get a prominent guest star to appear in it, and he can do this only if the role offered the actor is also prominent. If you will look back over the welter of plays on the air you will realize that the ones you remember are the *Miracle Worker's* and the *Marty's* and the *Maverick's,* shows built around one central character. They offered parts that actors pant to play.

Almost any subject can be treated so that the emphasis is on one character. He or she does not have to be before the camera constantly, he may not indeed have the lion's share of the dialogue; but he is the lead, he is memorable, he is vivid, and the audience must care more about what happens to him than about the fates of the other characters. Even in an instance of a play or film which nominally concerns several people, one character stands out: *Streetcar* is about Blanche, *Little Sheba* is about Lola, *Little Foxes* is about Regina. The exceptions, where it is not easy to extract from the group a single person more important than the rest—a *Grand Hotel,* an *Iceman Cometh,* or an *Outward Bound*—are very seldom found on popular television programs. There isn't time in an hour or a half hour to do justice to six or more equally prominent characters, and there isn't enough money in the budget to engage the superior actors who can play them.

You are going to find that it's easier and more satisfactory to devise your story so that one character dominates. Developing a theme with several people equally important can degenerate into a clever feat of juggling.

The star principal holds good for an anthology but also for a series with continuing characters. In the latter case you either tell a story in which a running, week-after-week character has the star part—*Columbo* or *Kojak* or *Marcus Welby, M.D.*—or you relegate the permanent lead to a secondary part and turn your plot-light on the guest star. When the story belongs to the character who comes from outside, then the series show becomes more like an anthology. Stars who have found rewarding parts in television films whose other actors appear every week range from Helen Traubel to Mickey Rooney.

The Far-Out Story

A question that relates to getting guest stars is: how far is it wise to go in picking unusual subject matter for an established series? A new kind of character may appeal to a producer because, if it's showy enough, it will attract a star who would turn down a conventional part. On the other hand, you may run afoul of sponsor taboos if you come up with something too exotic in the character line. Before you spend time on a story in which Edward, Prince of Wales, comes to the far west and meets Matt Dillon, or a segment for *Kung Fu* about beautiful Siamese twins, you had better inquire of the show's story editor if he is disposed to consider the subject you have devised.

But startling subject material can be a newcomer's best way to break into an established program and, as we shall shortly see, an old show is a new writer's best bet. A show whose rating has started to slip needs a blood transfusion, and the new blood can be the kind of story the producer has never done. Maybe it's a tour de force offering opportunities for wide publicity—a story with only two characters, or with only one character, or without dialogue.

In its third year *77 Sunset Strip*, with a dwindling audience, bought a story in which its week-after-week detective hero was literally the only character. True, there was a villain in this particular film who was dedicated to killing Private Eye Stu Bailey, but we never saw Stu's opponent, only heard his voice on the self-operating recording machine which was one of the many weird contraptions in the ghost town where the sleuth had been lured and trapped. For a self-conscious stab at novelty, this solo character sketch was surprisingly entertaining. Another detective series with its day in the sun was *Burke's Law;* one of its bids for the unusual was a story in which the same actress played four sisters. And several years ago a picture was made without dialogue. It was not a silent movie in the traditional sense, there was plenty of naturalistic noise, but the long pursuit which comprised this melodrama had been conceived as pantomime, and nobody talked.

So occasionally a far-out, bizarre story idea can be profitably exploited on a series show. But before you start trying to exploit it, make contact with the story editor and assure yourself that your revolutionary concept won't meet with instant resistance.

Snares and Pitfalls

Technical mistakes creep into screenplays, even by veterans, and you should be on guard against the solecisms that occur most frequently. In our workshop the mechanical mistakes tend to be made not during the first few weeks, when the camera directions are unfamiliar and everybody is concentrating on getting them right, but later on when the writer feels he has mastered the terms. He isn't paying as much attention. And having made a technical error, he probably won't catch it in rereading his copy because his editing is apt to be concerned only with his dialogue and the actions of his characters.

Blatant technical errors in a teleplay are distracting to the editor who is either going to accept your script or turn it down. The story may be superb but if the editor comes across too many camera puzzlers that make him stop and wonder, his attention is liable to be permanently diverted and you will lose a sale. I mentioned a student's confusion about POV SHOT and REVERSE ANGLE. Here is the way that confusion, if it gets into the teleplay, affects the reader. I am in the middle of a tense scene about a girl alone in a spooky house at night:

```
INT. LIVING ROOM    MED. CLOSE SHOT    FAITH

Faith opens the drawer of the old desk and starts to search
through it. Suddenly she stiffens as she hears a SOUND from
the direction of the window. It is a high, piercing, sus-
tained squeak like the screech of a long finger nail being
drawn down a blackboard.

She slams the drawer shut and runs to the window as CAMERA
HOLDS on her back.


REVERSE ANGLE

On the road beyond the garden, plainly visible in the moon-
light, a procession of six hooded figures moves slowly
along. In the forefront a man in a long cloak is blowing on
a fife making the weird SOUND which attracted Faith's at-
tention.
```

The sound isn't the only weird thing about this scene. The first direction explicitly tells us we are looking at Faith's back when she is at the window. Cutting to a REVERSE ANGLE means we are now looking in the reverse direction—at her face. It would be perfectly appropriate to follow the first direction with a true reverse angle, since a close-up showing Faith's fear or bewilderment would be in keeping. But instead of the expected shot, we look across the garden from her view-point. Instead of REVERSE ANGLE the shot heading should be either FAITH'S POV or WHAT SHE SEES. A small matter indeed, but sufficient to break the reader's concentration, to bother him at a moment when he should be utterly absorbed.

Here are a few other common mistakes, culled from students' work and also from the screenplays of experienced writers who tend to become sloppy now and then:

Forgetting to come out of a shot. We cut from a medium shot of two people taking to a close-up of one, and then continue the dialogue for maybe a page or more without bothering to write that we are back in a two shot. If the directions were followed, we would be looking at the features of one person while heaven only knows what is going on around him. Or we cut to an insert of an object and neglect to write BACK TO SCENE after the object has been established.

Forgetting to indicate at the beginning of a new sequence whether it is day or night.

Writing LONG SHOT at the beginning of a scene and neglecting to indicate a closer shot for the action and dialogue that follow.

Writing ANOTHER ANGLE when a completely new camera subject is introduced. ANOTHER ANGLE always means a different view of the *same subject.* It can, of course, be sufficiently different to include something in the shot that was not visible before. For instance, suppose we are in a close-up of Faith. In a close-up little else is visible. We want to show the door opening behind Faith, so we go to ANOTHER ANGLE. But that means Faith is still in view. If we wanted to show the door opening in a shot that did *not* have Faith in it, we would have to write MED. SHOT DOOR or ANGLE ON DOOR. The subject of the previous shot must always be seen somewhere or other in the shot you label ANOTHER ANGLE.

Ending a scene by writing DISSOLVE TO and then beginning the following scene on the next page with the direction FADE IN. There seems to be no reason for setting down such an impossible contradiction, but it happens with depressing frequency. A similar but relatively venial piece of forgetfulness is fading out on one scene and neglecting to FADE IN on the next.

Omitting camera movements in the description of happenings that occur at some distance from each other. A recent example in the script of a feature film professed to show the legs (only) of a man lying on a bed, his mistress on the other side of the room combing her hair, birds twittering in a tree outside the window of a third wall, and the lady's husband suddenly appearing in the doorway in a fourth location. Even Cinerama couldn't do this in a stationary shot. The direction should tell us that the Camera PANS from one person to another. And remember the convenient blanket term for describing movement all over the set in one shot: CAMERA FOLLOWS ACTION.

Be simple and restrained in your use of camera directions and you will stay out of trouble. Thoroughly understand any terms you do use. That way you will never write anything like the incredible description a new writer once composed for a historical movie at 20th Century-Fox: "And now we DISSOLVE all the way around the table from Queen Victoria to Gladstone to Disraeli."

The Need for Simplicity

Descriptive passages in a teleplay should be easily understandable. Writers who practice directness and clarity in their dialogue occasionally "spread themselves" in their directions. The teleplay's the thing and elaborate prose doesn't belong in it. You may get a story editor with the time to be appreciative of the embroidered descriptive passage, but the chances aren't good.

The two main things to avoid, and they both come under the head of self-indulgence, are a display of erudition and the attempt to be clever. Cleverness turns out too often to be facetiousness, and a parade of recondite knowledge tends to annoy producers. If one of them reads a direction in your teleplay that says, "The vicar drives up in a stanhope," he may know what you mean, but it would be wiser and seemlier to write, "The vicar drives up in a light, two-wheeled carriage drawn by two horses, the English country vehicle commonly called a stanhope."

A whimsical sense of humor, likewise, may result in harm. I once came across this direction in a scene that was supposed to be suspenseful: "Halfway down the corridor he pauses as he hears a strange noise in the distance. He cannot identify the noise. It might be a woman's scream, or the howl of a wild beast, or a voice calling out, 'Alabama casts forty-four votes for Oscar W. Underwood!'" Such fantastic japes are all very well in their place, but to come unexpectedly on one in a television script that is not primarily comedy can seriously unnerve a producer.

The Place of Comedy

Is there a place for comedy relief in a television script that is not essentially funny? Many writers have pondered over the advisability of putting humor into a drama or melodrama that runs no longer than an hour. There is no covering answer since so much depends on the kind of characters you are working with. But it is impossible not to be struck by the absence of a leavening humor in the majority of serious hour or half-hour shows. The tradition of comedy relief in the popular theater is long established: plays and movies designed to take up a whole evening have the time and the space for it, and the writer seldom wants to sustain a solemn mood unbroken for two hours and a half.

When you have only thirty or sixty minutes, minus time out for commercials, to tell a story, create characters, and build a mood of suspense and excitement, there seems to be no time for comedy. It is certainly much easier not to bother with it when the main line of your story is something else, and since most scripts are written in haste the abandonment of humor shows signs of becoming the convention.

There are refreshing exceptions. They are found in teleplays whose dimensional characters have grotesque, eccentric, original facets to their natures from which fun spontaneously springs. In creating television drama, then, you will be on solid ground if comedy comes easily and naturally from within the personalities of your people; if humor at a given point seems inevitable, if it is not laid on from the outside, if you feel that a character must do or say something resulting in laughter or else be untrue to his nature, then it *belongs*. The great master of comedy in grim circumstances is Sean O'Casey. The magnificent comic outbursts of *The Plough and the Stars* go hand in hand with the horrors of the Easter Rising in Dublin, but they are so essentially expressions of the characters that comedy, rather than being a mere relief from tragedy, becomes tragedy's other face: tragedy and comedy are equally valid parts of a dramatic whole. You would do very well to consult O'Casey's plays (*Juno and the Paycock* and *Red Roses For Me* are two that share this comedy-as-a-part-of tragedy quality) as models for comedy of character in a serious story frame.

The Importance of the Image

Review your work and see if you can find any places where dialogue is performing the task that should be allotted to action. Can a crisis in your teleplay be made more effective by showing it instead of talking it out? This check on how you are using the cinema medium is a vital part of the inventory.

We won't labor this point because it was covered in Chapter IV, when we learned what comprised the motion picture form, and saw in the example from *Becket* how a happening became more dramatically compelling when it could be shown instead of recited. But another illustration that stems from Chapter VII, where dialogue was our only consideration, will reenforce the principle.

Turn back to the turbulent tale of Gerald and Ingrid whose infant vanished while Gerald was in the supermarket. The atrocious unbroken speech in which Gerald announced the kidnapping was correctly junked for the passage of dialogue between husband and wife that was more natural and dynamic. But when we look at the story elements as more than a narrow exercise in dialogue, we must ask: shouldn't the abduction be seen rather than heard of? I think so. This is a crisis which demands to be seen by the audience. Let us show Gerald driving into the parking lot at the market. He makes sure the child is securely strapped in his seat, assures him that daddy won't be long, and enters the store. We see him pick up his can of corn syrup (I am supposing that we want to keep the actual abduction a mystery), perhaps exchange a pleasantry with the checker, and return to the car —and discover the little boy missing and the strap cut.

From here on, we could do one of a number of things. We could continue to show events in sequence. Gerald calls the police, they arrive, the search is on, and after being questioned Gerald drives home to break the news. As he leaves, we could dissolve to the home where he has finished telling Ingrid what has happened, thus sidestepping unnecessary exposition. Or, having pictured the main happening, we could make a drastic but perfectly acceptable time jump, and dissolve from Gerald's discovery that the baby is missing to the home after the police have arrived and are questioning both Gerald and his wife. Or we might conclude that this is a good place to use a shock cut. Gerald rushes to the phone in the market, and we hear him say to the operator, "I want the police!" CUT TO Gerald and Ingrid at their home, with Gerald saying, "I called them. They got there right away." And on with the scene.

Whatever are the details of the progression after Gerald finds the child missing, we will have accomplished the main thing: written this part of the story for a *film*.

New Ink in Old Bottles

Does the new writer stand a better chance if he writes a story for a new program or for one that has been on the air several years?

This is a pertinent question. If somebody in the workshop fails to ask it (but somebody usually does) I bring it up myself. At first glance you may be tempted to favor the brand new show. Its producers are breaking new ground, surely they must be eager for story material, and they should be cordial to the new writer who shows promise and whom, perhaps, they can develop into a dependable contributor to the program. The old show, on the other hand, will probably have attracted well-known writers into its orbit and consequently won't be as interested in new talent. The reasoning here is plausible, but the premise shakes.

By the time the public hears about a new television program, before it gets on the air, an immense amount of work has been done on the project. Its creator and his associates have mapped out stories, assigned writers they have often worked with to develop others, and made tentative commitments for more story material if the program survives the critical period, its first thirteen weeks on the air, after which it will be renewed or canceled, according to the response from the public as interpreted by the Nielsen rating. Unless they are very badly organized, they will not be searching for stories at this time.

Even if this were not the situation, you would be handicapped in trying to devise a story for a series about which you know little except, say, that it is an action melodrama about an army post in New Mexico around the turn of the century and its leading characters are a young officer from West Point and his bride. You would need much more information obtainable only from conferences with the producer, and I am afraid a producer who is launching a new show reserves his time for writers he knows.

In contrast to this discouraging prospect, look at the show going into its fourth year. Its producer has made more than a hundred pictures during the past three seasons. He is having trouble getting stories that haven't been done before. The writers he has depended on become stale, start to repeat themselves. If the show is to stay on the air, it must have new blood. That blood may very well come from an unknown writer who has seen the program enough to be familiar with it but is sufficiently detached from its grind to create unusual characters in situations which, although perhaps not original, are seen in a new light and treated in interesting and unconventional fashion.

I have a friend who made his first television sale to such a show. Unfortunately, the series expired before he could take advantage of his script's favorable reception and submit another. Shortly afterwards, the producer of the canceled program was assigned to develop another series for the same network. My friend, Bob, on the basis of his one sale to a moribund show, was one of the writers called in by the producer and briefed about the new project: he wrote three of the teleplays for the first thirteen films.

Instant success like Bob's is not the norm, but many writers do establish themselves in television by first channeling their submissions into the old shows desperate for new stories. Offhand, I can think of nobody who forced his way into the field through a new program which he had never seen.

Leaving Things Out

There is a trap so obvious that nine out of ten writers don't recognize it; but nine out of ten, at one time or another, fall into it. It is a failure to communicate, a failure to make clear to the reader what is crystal clear to the writer. It may be leaving out a line of description, or the omission of four words of dialogue, or a hastily written phrase in dialogue or directions that causes the sense to be ambiguous. Like the wrong use of a camera term it can result in disaster: the reader is puzzled, the spell is broken, the virtues of the story line are abruptly severed by an attack of meaninglessness.

It can happen when you have been working very hard over a sequence. The scene was not right to start with, it didn't "flow" properly. You wrote it over and over again. It improved and finally, hours later, you were satisfied. You were also—by this time—so immersed in your characters and their behavior that their every move and every utterance were seen and heard on the private movie screen in your head. When a writer reaches this point, it is inconceivable to him that the words he has written can fail to reproduce for his reader the same detail that they do for him. If he has unwittingly left out a link in the chain, he subconsciously "makes allowance" for the elision. He honestly thinks it is there when it isn't.

This accident is also prone to happen when you are dealing with complexities of character or situation. If your character is acting in a devious fashion, deceiving his companions but not deceiving the audience, be very careful that your description of his behavior makes sense. I recall an instance from the first draft of a script by an experienced writer who was no more proof against this misfortune than you are. His leading character was a nightclub entertainer named Max, a handsome, personable fellow who had prevailed upon a beautiful young singer, Yvonne, to run off to Mexico with him. For very good reasons Yvonne wanted no word of the elopement to leak out, and Max swore that nobody would know of it until after their marriage. As the couple are waiting in a Nevada hotel for Max's private plane to be readied, he excuses himself to call his agent and goes into a phone booth. But instead of reaching his agent, he calls a gossip columnist and tells him everything about the elopement. This is a shock: the leading man is revealing himself as a publicity-hungry doublecrosser. So far apparently so good. In the next scene the couple hear the columnist broadcasting. Max is stunned when the columnist says he got his story from Max. He is genuinely astonished and outraged because he had told the columnist not to reveal how he got the story, to attribute it to somebody else.

Now the trouble here is that the teleplay in its first version did not have the line of dialogue in the phone booth from Max to the columnist: "Whatever you do, don't say you got the story from me—remember, you heard it somewhere else." The writer was so intent on the surprise effect of his scene, revealing that Max who had sworn secrecy is suddenly and callously breaking the promise, that he forgot to put in everything he should have. Consequently, Max's shock when he discovers that the columnist has pinned the revelation on him after all, is pretty puzzling to the reader who can't recall that Max demanded any such promise.

A dangerous sin of omission is neglecting to make clear in dialogue what may be clear in directions. You impart information to the person reading the script but fail to impart it to the eventual audience. This kind of mistake can get past more than one person. For example:

```
CLOSE SHOT    GALBRAITH

Galbraith stands lost in thought, trying to fit the pieces
of this puzzle together. It is unlike Carson to kidnap a
child and he doesn't understand this new development.
```

What Galbraith does immediately afterwards is determined by his knowledge that Carson is unlikely to kidnap a child. Galbraith's actions, therefore, would be perfectly clear to the person *reading* the script but confusing to the viewer of the picture who does not possess this small piece of information.

To guard against these mistakes, be sure you are cool and detached when you edit your copy. If you have had a struggle with a scene, if it has "come right" only after a lot of thought and work, put it aside and do something else. Leave it, if possible, until the next day. Then you will be objective, you will not be a prey to the blind spots that cause these breakdowns in communication, and you will be able to detect instantly the absence of the key line which tells your audience that Marie Antoinette's necklace is indeed missing.

VALEDICTORY

In concluding this book I shall leave you with a universal question to ponder. In this chapter we have dealt with problems that "face many writers" or "involve most of you." There were solutions. But here is one that faces every drama writer; every one, that is, who has a smidgin of conscientiousness and responsibility about his work.

There is no satisfactory solution.

It is not a new problem. It is the concern, the very proper concern, about what other people will do to the writer's work.

I have before me a letter from a student. It arrived two days after a workshop inventory session. This young writer had hesitated to spread out before the class the subject that was on her mind. It represented a rather personal kind of worry; perhaps she was being whimsical and unprofessional to let it obsess her. After protesting, then, that her problem might be nothing more than a private neurosis, she proceeded to speak up for every drama writer in the world:

> I remember when I first started, my biggest problem, or so I thought, was not knowing when to dissolve or fade out or cut; not knowing how many spaces came between this and that, and whether this and that should be in caps or not, etc., etc. . . .
>
> Then when I began to surmount these things (which really weren't as bad as I'd feared, sort of like learning multiplication tables) I began to be afraid that maybe I didn't have the ability to write a teleplay. By this I don't mean that I was insecure about my ability to write. I convinced myself that I could do that long ago—right or wrong—or I wouldn't have

stuck to it so long. But I mean I was afraid that plays—and teleplays specifically—weren't my forte. My first play seemed endless. About Page 35 I was convinced that I'd never finish it and if I did it would be abominable. But I did finish it and it wasn't abominable.

Now that I'm writing my third hour teleplay, and the two problems I just mentioned no longer bug me, something else has really started to get me down. I'll try to explain it—if I can.

I tried to pick a good theme, something I believed in, so that when and if it were ever actually produced people would be moved by it or made to think or made mad—or that some emotion would result. I tried to fit my theme into a show, to keep it within that show's format, and still say what I wanted to say in an effective way. Then having come to the next stage—getting into actual teleplay—I searched for the precise words, in the precise tense, precisely singular or plural, understandable symbols, and easily communicable expressions, etc. (that's a horribly unbalanced sentence). The effectiveness of one whole scene hinges on the fact that I used the singular of *birds* rather than the plural. Another on whether a man is only insensitive or plain mean. Now you're wondering what the hell I'm driving at. It's this: is it really going to make any difference at all? I mean, if I ever do get this thing produced, is somebody going to think it doesn't make any difference and say "birds" instead of "bird"? Is some tired actor or harassed director going to characterize my man as "mean" rather than "insensitive"? Is what I'm trying to say ever going to be heard, even if it's actually produced? Does it make any difference, at all?

Yes, it makes a difference. The question raised by this letter is a staggering one for its writer and for every other writer in the challenging realm of the theater, whatever its form may be.

Yes. "Bird" is liable to become "birds." Your carefully constructed, insensitive character may well be played by an actor who will make him the meanest dog-heavy this side of Al Capp's Dogpatch. You do well to worry about these things. All of you.

But as long as you worry about your writing you need not worry about yourself as a writer.

There are two observations to be made about this expression of concern. The first is a piece of practical advice. It is detailed in Chapter VI where we looked at the relationship between the writer and the director. Cultivating the director, working with him when you can, is the best way to insure that your work gets on the screen as you want it to. The changes will be made by you. At the worst they will not come as a shock.

The other observation? If you have the same fears about what will happen to your work as Betty Langdon had, then you are reacting in the only way a true writer can. Lacking those fears, you are a hack. Hang on to them. Don't let the changes that will be made in your work dishearten you, or create in you the who-cares-so-long-as-they-pay-me attitude that is the enemy of honest writing. Stick to your principles. And be sure the typewriter ribbon is black and the carbon paper fresh. Good luck.

APPENDIX

A COMPLETE TELEPLAY SCRIPT

APPENDIX

A Complete Teleplay Script

Question: What Is Truth? by JAMES E. MOSER. Pilot teleplay for Mr. Moser's television series, *Slattery's People.*

The hour-length teleplay *Question: What Is Truth?*, reproduced here in its final revised version as it was ready to go before the cameras, is notable on several counts. It is the pilot (the introductory show of a series) of a filmed program on the CBS network entitled *Slattery's People,* which won critical approval during the 1964 and 1965 seasons. *Slattery's People* is of course designed for popular entertainment, but it has stature and dignity because it is about something important: the workings of state government. Its qualities of dramatic storytelling and penetrating characterization are nowhere more strikingly evident than in this first script.

Slattery's creator and executive producer, James E. Moser, is a veteran of television, well known for *Dragnet, Medic,* and *Ben Casey,* programs which he originated and many of whose individual segments he wrote.

The state capitol, around and in which the *Slattery* stories take place, is never identified and we are never told in which state Slattery is a representative, but the setting is no dream world. Before he wrote the first teleplay of the series, Moser researched his subject for eight months in Sacramento; the procedure of the legislature closely resembles that of California's, and many of the scenes in *Slattery* were photographed in Sacramento.

Every principle that you have been studying is illustrated in

Question: What Is Truth? Its mechanics are impeccable: you will find all the directions from Fade In to Fade Out correctly used. Dialogue scenes are permitted to play out uninterrupted by camera indications, the shifts from close shots to medium ones and the incidental movement of the camera being properly left to the director's discretion. However, when the author sets down a scene the visual progression of which he regards as important (as in the opening scenes in the House Chamber), he meticulously describes camera movement and the sequence of shots he wishes used. The attentive student will be aware throughout his reading of this teleplay of the writer's sense of responsibility to the director in putting down the story. He will also be aware—in such areas as the dialogue scenes mentioned—of the writer's refusal to usurp responsibility not his.

Technically, then, *Question: What Is Truth?* is a thoroughly professional teleplay. What concerns us even more is its admirable dramatic structure. I shall not attempt a step-by-step analysis of its adherence to primary principles, for if you have studied the early chapters of the book you will have no difficulty in discovering for yourself such things as how the critical dramatic problem is shaped by elements in Slattery's character, how growth is constant in the happenings of the narrative, and the relation the climax has to the series of crises that have led up to it.

I shall, however, direct your attention to the treatment of exposition and preparation in the early sequences. It is difficult to recall any other teleplay in which the author posed himself an equally complex problem of exposition and then solved it with such skill and dispatch. In addition to the exposition native to a drama with only the usual amount of complications, Moser had some explaining to do about his subject. You may contend, if you like, that we all *should* understand the workings of our state assemblies; the fact is many of us in the television audience have only a hazy, imprecise knowledge of local government. When the hero of a teleplay is a state assemblyman, the audience had better be told immediately what it is he does and why it is important. The environment in which he works must also be quickly established.

The plot proper of this first teleplay in the *Slattery* series begins at the top of script page 8 when the newspaperman, Radcliff, receives the press release that will spark Slattery's explosive investigation. By that time we have been given our bearings in the State House of Representatives, we have watched Slattery working with his colleagues, and we have been shown the kind of business that concerns him as his amendments to a bill are debated. Nor is this all. Slattery's clash with the majority floor leader tells us a great deal about our hero: he is poised, aggressive, has a sharp wit, and is not to be caught napping. Within these first seven pages, too, Slattery's old friend and future opponent—the script's second most important character—is introduced and pointedly characterized. This vital exposition and scene-setting take place dynamically, conflict bursts out, and the audience is being involved and entertained as it absorbs information. Preparation and exposition go on after the real story begins, both being adroitly threaded into the developing incident. Slattery continues his professional activities. This phase of the exposition—showing us how Slattery operates and just what his job consists of—is enhanced by a slight shock which avoids the expected: Slattery does not win his amendment fight, he is roundly trounced by a House vote.

You will derive maximum benefit from the *Slattery* teleplay if you constantly use it as a reference. During the study of this book, check the script for usages of those principles discussed in the text. The opening pages of the teleplay, as we have just seen, provide an excellent example of manipulating exposition according to the methods suggested in Chapter III. Here is another principle illustrated:

At the close of Chapter I we talked about the shock cut—how you can ignore time and space and go instantaneously from one scene to another for heightened dramatic effect and to eliminate nonessentials. Examine *Question: What Is Truth?* and you will quickly find, on page 21, an apt use of shock cutting. Moser ends one scene with a group of legislators deciding that one of their group must be investigated. The last line of the scene, spoken by the object of the impending probe, is "Turn the bloodhounds loose." The author cuts instantly to Slattery, some time later, in the middle of a violent protest against his appointment as head of that investigating committee.

QUESTION: WHAT IS TRUTH?

by

James E. Moser

pilot teleplay for SLATTERY'S PEOPLE

SLATTERY'S PEOPLE

1. QUESTION: WHAT IS TRUTH?

FADE IN:

1. INT. HOUSE CHAMBER - DAY

CAMERA OPENS on a BIG CLOSE SHOT of the voting mechanism on Slattery's desk. MUSIC HITS SHARPLY, STACCATO. The sound is brilliant, arresting, important, but very brief. MUSIC CUTS OFF ABRUPTLY as we hear the usual SOUNDS of the House in session: much activity, much urgent talking o.s. Slattery's hand comes into frame, he inserts a key into the voting mechanism, turns it, then flips back the cover revealing two small all-important black buttons. One is labeled "YES"...the other, "NO". CAMERA PULLS BACK SLIGHTLY and we can make out the name typed on a white card which has been inserted into a small, rectangular metal bracket fixed to the front of the desk. It reads simply: "MR. SLATTERY".

CAMERA NOW PANS QUICKLY UP and PAST the rostrum, UP and OVER the national and state flags (the latter not identifiable) which flank the rostrum, UP and OVER the large and imposing legend lettered on the wall directly behind and above the Speaker's stand: POPULI VOLUNTAS LEGITIME UNICA REGENDI RADIX. Without pausing for translation or explanation, CAMERA PANS UP and OVER the legend and HOLDS on a huge, gilt-framed portrait of Thomas Jefferson. MUSIC PUNCTUATES AGAIN...BRIEFLY, ARRESTINGLY. As CAMERA PULLS BACK SLOWLY for a FULL DOWN SHOT of the entire House chamber, we hear:

VOICE (o.s.)
Democracy is a very bad form of government. But I ask you never to forget... all the others are so much worse.

There is a sudden flurry of activity down on the floor as CAMERA HOLDS for a moment on the FULL DOWN SHOT of the floor and then starts to DESCEND QUICKLY as the MAIN TITLE is SUPERIMPOSED: SLATTERY'S PEOPLE.

(NOTE: The pacing and movement in the ensuing sequence must be snappy, crisp, vital, all business-like... no dawdling, no lingering.)

CAMERA MOVES SWIFTLY IN for a CLOSE SHOT of the Call-Board in the Assistant Sergeants-at-Arms box at the rear of the House chamber. We see the number "7" flashing brightly and insistently on the board. CAMERA PULLS

(CONTINUED)

2.

1 CONTINUED

BACK SLIGHTLY revealing a young SERGEANT-AT-ARMS as he suddenly snaps his head around, takes a note of the flashing signal, rises quickly and exits the box, CAMERA PANNING WITH HIM. CAMERA FOLLOWS BEHIND HIM as he makes his way quickly across the rear aisle of the chamber, then turns and starts down the main aisle towards his objective. There is the same flurry of motion and activity as we observed previously. The youthful figure makes his way through the throng of members to a desk near the front of the House chamber. He confers briefly with the occupant of the desk (whom we cannot recognize because his BACK IS TO CAMERA), then he is handed an envelope. He turns and EXITS scene quickly. CAMERA HOLDS on the occupant of the desk as he reaches forward and grasps his microphone stand.

DIRECT CUT TO:

2 INT. FRONT OF HOUSE CHAMBER

CAMERA SHOOTING UP toward the ceiling as Slattery's mike is suddenly flipped upward into frame. A small light attached to the arm of the mike flashes on. A deep-throated gong SOUNDS throughout the chamber. THEME MUSIC UP BIG, mingling with the varied SOUNDS of the House as it is placed under "call". CAMERA PANS SWIFTLY to the rear of the chamber as the huge 15-foot doors are slowly swung shut and locked. CAMERA also takes care to NOTE a red light to one side of the doors which is flashing insistently and a buzzer just below it SOUNDING intermittently.

DIRECT CUT TO:

3 INT. SIDE ENTRANCE TO HOUSE CHAMBER - DAY

CAMERA FEATURING a different alarm bell and flashing light which continue IN ACTION until the side doors are swung shut and locked. CAMERA SWINGS AROUND in a FULL-ABOUT-FACE and starts to MOVE ACROSS the chamber. Immediately we PICK UP SLATTERY as he moves determinedly from his desk to the rostrum where he converses briefly with the CLERK who then hands him a copy of the roll call. Slattery turns, starts back toward his desk as he peruses the roll call. He stops abruptly, glances up from the scrap of paper he holds, looks intently across the floor of the House as if searching for a particular face. In a brief moment his eyes indicate he's located the man he seeks and he starts threading his way resolutely down the crowded aisle.

(CONTINUED)

3.

3 CONTINUED

NOTE: DURING THE COURSE OF THE PRECEDING SCENES, THE FOLLOWING WILL BE SUPERIMPOSED INDIVIDUALLY AT THE APPROPRIATE PLACES:

MAIN TITLE - SLATTERY'S PEOPLE

CREATED BY - James E. Moser

STARRING - Richard Crenna

FADE OUT

FADE IN:

4 INT. CAPITOL, THIRD FLOOR CORRIDOR

It's just after the opening of the daily session of the House and traffic is heavy along the corridor. CAMERA FOLLOWS FRANK RADCLIFF, HOLDING on his back as he weaves his way through the throng on his way to the main entrance of the House chamber. As he approaches the towering 15-foot double doors which lead in the House we see the entrance is attended by TWO ASSISTANT SERGEANTS-AT-ARMS, their glistening gold lapel badges much in evidence. Radcliff nods a brief silent 'good morning' to one of the Sergeants-at-Arms and enters without pausing.

5 INT. HOUSE CHAMBER - DAY

CAMERA FEATURING Radcliff as he enters and starts to make his way toward one of the press desks set against one of the walls about midway in the chamber. It is now we see Radcliff's face for the first time. A veteran capital correspondent for a big city newspaper, The Times-Chronicle, Frank Radcliff is an affable, intent, quite dedicated man in his early 50's. As for his dress, well, he's hardly sloppy but you also know at first glance he'll never be nominated for a sartorial award.

Radcliff carries a folded newspaper and a well-thumbed notebook under one arm as CAMERA FOLLOWS HIM to his desk. It may be well to note here that since we entered the chamber with Radcliff the House has been in session. And in addition to the usual amount of activity, desk-hopping, etc., one of the House members... specifically the Majority Floor Leader, REPRESENTATIVE CARL BUTLER, has been in the midst of an address to his fellow colleagues. As Radcliff reaches his desk, which sports a name-plate reading TIMES-CHRONICLE, he tosses his papers down and glances off in Carl Butler's direction. CAMERA PANS

(CONTINUED)

4.

5 CONTINUED

QUICKLY with his glance and HOLDS on Butler as he continues speaking. (NOTE: THE ENSUING SPEECH WILL START BACK FROM THE FIRST MOMENT WE ENTERED THE CHAMBER.)

BUTLER
(as if continuing)
... And by way of conclusion, ladies and gentlemen of the House, I'm sure you are quite aware that there are seated in this chamber certain parties who have been playing "games", so to speak, with this valuable piece of legislation. And the "games" these people have been playing... one party in particular... I am sure disgust you every bit as much as they disgust me. Is this person so blinded by his conceit that he believes we don't know what's going on? Does he think we're so stupid that we don't realize what he's up to in proposing these amendments? If so, then let me assure him in the name of the membership of this House that he is tragically mistaken.

6 ANOTHER ANGLE - THE HOUSE CHAMBER

CAMERA HOLDING on Butler in the b.g. as he continues. In the immediate f.g., the long, collapsible arm of the microphone stand on Slattery's desk is flung up into frame and the small light which is attached near the end of the arm flashes on after a second or two.

BUTLER
(continuing)
Gentlemen, let us show this man once and for all that there is no room for ruthless political maneuverings in this chamber.

Slattery moves into frame, grasps the arm of the microphone. He's quietly angry but it's evident he has full control of himself.

SLATTERY
Mister Speaker?

Up on the rostrum, the Speaker, tough, iron-jawed BERT METCAFF, turns his attention to Slattery.

(CONTINUED)

5.

6 CONTINUED

METCAFF
Mister Slattery, for what purpose do you rise?

SLATTERY
Mister Speaker, will you inquire if the honorable member from Pierce County will yield for a question?

METCAFF
Will you yield?

BUTLER
(bit annoyed)
Yes... all right.

SLATTERY
(evenly)
Mister Butler, I'm sure there's no doubt in anyone's mind who you're referring to, so I can only assume you've forgotten my name. It's Slattery, Mister Butler. S-L-A-T-T-E-R-Y.

A moderate wave of laughter sweeps the floor.

METCAFF
Your remarks are not in order, Mister Slattery. Do you have a question or don't you?

SLATTERY
(simply)
Yes sir. I'd like to know if Mister Butler knows my name.

BUTLER
Unfortunately, sir... I know it only too well.

SLATTERY
(snaps quickly)
Then why don't you use it? This is a state legislature, not a prep school debating squad.

As Speaker Metcaff gavels once, Slattery quickly pulls down his mike stand and takes his seat. Metcaff frowns darkly in his direction, then turns and nods to Butler.

METCAFF
Proceed, Mister Butler.

(CONTINUED)

6.

6 CONTINUED - (2):

Butler's uncomfortable. There's little or nothing more he can say. Strategically he's smart enough to know the best thing for him to do is close briefly and sit down. He does just that.

BUTLER
I'm not going to belabor you, gentlemen. This bill, as it stands, merits your full support. I strongly urge a "No" vote on Mister Slattery's proposed amendments.

Butler sits down, lowering his mike as he does so.

7 MED. CLOSE SHOT - SLATTERY

as he sits at his desk, frowning at a couple of tally cards, trying to figure out how many votes he has going for and against him. Immediately REPRESENTATIVE HARRY SANBORN moves up beside the desk. Sanborn is in his late 50's... virile, white-haired, affable, rather handsome, an experienced, veteran legislator... tough, honored, respected. He and Slattery are close friends despite the fact they belong to opposing political parties.

SANBORN
(grinning)
Shape up, Slattery. There's no room for political maneuvering in this chamber.

SLATTERY
(he's forced to grin)
How are you, Harry.

SANBORN
Ought to be ashamed, needling poor old Butler like that.
(bends over to study Slattery's tally cards)
Things could be better, huh? How do you count it?

SLATTERY
33 with me... 36 against. 5 abstaining... 6 absentees.

(CONTINUED)

7 CONTINUED

SANBORN
(grunts)
So we need five votes.
(turns to go)
Well, let's see if I can
do you any good.

CAMERA FOLLOWS Sanborn to his desk only a few yards away where he raises his mike. The light on the mike stand goes on. Slattery is still framed in the f.g.

METCAFF (o.s.)
For what purpose do you rise,
Mr. Sanborn.

SANBORN
Mister Speaker, I rise in
support of Mister Slattery's
amendments to the bill.

METCAFF (o.s.)
You have the floor, Mister
Sanborn.

As Sanborn starts to speak, CAMERA TURNS to HOLD Slattery and JOHNNY in a TWO SHOT. JOHNNY RAMOS, who has just walked up to Slattery's desk, is Slattery's youthful, good-looking assistant. He is one of the corps of ambitious young men in the state capital known as Legislative Interns. Sanborn's voice in the b.g., o.s., is audible but not readable.

JOHNNY
Y'know, for two guys on opposite
sides of the fence you and
Sanborn get along pretty well.

SLATTERY
He happens to be a good friend.

8 CAMERA FEATURING RADCLIFF

checking a sheaf of papers on his desk. A young SECRETARY comes by, nods, places a three-page mimeographed press release on his desk and moves on. Radcliff picks it up, glances at it casually and is about to file it in the waste basket when he suddenly does a double-take, hurriedly reads through the release to get the gist of it and reacts with much interest and much concern. For a newspaperman this is a blockbuster of a story and his expression shows it. He glances across the chamber.

9 ANOTHER ANGLE - THE HOUSE CHAMBER

as Harry Sanborn finishes his speech.

SANBORN
... and this being the case, fellow colleagues, I cannot urge you too strongly to cast an "aye" vote on the amendments proposed by Mister Slattery. Thank you.

Sanborn sits down, lowers his mike. Speaker Metcaff glances over the floor.

METCAFF
Does anyone else wish to speak on the proposed amendments?
(brief pause)
No further debate?
(brief pause)
Mister Slattery, you may close.

CAMERA FEATURES Slattery as he gets up, raises his mike, then turns to face the House membership.

SLATTERY
Mister Speaker... members of the House. I have offered these amendments for one reason and one reason only: to restore the bill now before you to a semblance of its former self... both in spirit and intent. I ask you to compare the original bill which was submitted all of two months ago with the measure now before you. And if you can find any significant similarities, well congratulations... your faculties are much keener than mine. The original bill has been so carved up, jumped on, jimmied with, sugar-coated and watered down that right now it means virtually nothing at all.

10 ANOTHER ANGLE - THE HOUSE CHAMBER

CAMERA FEATURES Frank Radcliff as he spots someone of great interest at the rear of the chamber. He quickly gets to his feet, grabs the recent press release off his desk, and heads toward the back of the chamber. Meantime, Slattery continues speaking o.s. Most of what we hear is not readable. CAMERA FOLLOWS Radcliff back to a spot near the Sergeants-at-Arms box where he moves up to SENATOR BART ELLIOTT who stands conversing quietly and very earnestly with House Majority Leader Carl Butler. Elliott, a freshman senator, is about 28, able, well-dressed, egotistical and very ambitious. As Radcliff moves up to them it's apparent that Butler is angry, much disturbed with Elliott.

SLATTERY (o.s.)
(continuing)
The members of the Rev and Tax committee took care of that. And this is not a case, I assure you, of being petulant because a committee saw fit to amend a bill I co-authored. I have no use for cry-babies and I'm sure you don't. Compromise is a cardinal rule in our job and I've never disputed it. But whoever's responsible for emasculating this bill clearly doesn't want compromise. They want capitulation.

Radcliff nods briefly to Carl Butler as he moves up to them.

RADCLIFF
Carl...

BUTLER
(cautiously)
Oh... how are you, Frank?

Radcliff turns and extends a hand to Elliott.

RADCLIFF
I haven't had the pleasure so far this session, Senator, but my name's Frank Radcliff... with the Times-Chronicle.

(CONTINUED)

10.

10 CONTINUED

ELLIOTT
(immediately beam-
ing)
Oh, sure... glad to meet you,
Frank. It's a real pleasure.
What can I do for you?

RADCLIFF
(shows him press
release)
I just got this press handout
from your office. There's so
much dynamite in it I thought
I'd double-check and make sure
it was the real thing.

ELLIOTT
No mistake. It's the real thing.

RADCLIFF
(turns to leave)
Thank you, Senator... that's
all I wanted to know.

Radcliff moves off and Butler turns angrily to Elliott.

BUTLER
When did your office start
handing out that press release?

ELLIOTT
About half an hour ago.

BUTLER
Has the letter been sent over
to this side yet?

ELLIOTT
(nods to indicate)
It should be up there on the
desk right now.

11 INT. HOUSE CHAMBER - DAY

CAMERA FEATURING Slattery as he concludes his speech.

SLATTERY
This measure is important... it
is vital. Ladies and gentlemen
of the House... I ask for an
"aye" vote on the amendments.

12 MED. CLOSE SHOT - SLATTERY

as he sits down, lowering his mike. O.s. we HEAR:

METCAFF (o.s.)
All debate having been concluded, the question is on adoption of Mr. Slattery's amendments. A majority of those members present is required and a roll call has been requested. The clerk will prepare the roll.

We hear a soft GONG SOUND throughout the chamber signifying that the voting board is open. Slattery reaches over, firmly presses the "aye" button on the desk voting mechanism. In the b.g. we see scattered lights appear on the board as the voting starts. Sanborn moves up beside Slattery who is quick to note the older man's expression.

SLATTERY
Not one of my days, huh?

SANBORN
Not one of your better ones.

Slattery turns and looks up at the voting board, CAMERA PANNING WITH HIS GAZE. Most of the voting is completed.

SLATTERY
(looking up, counting)
... 35... 36... 38 no's. 33 ayes.
We've had it.
(grabs Sanborn's arm)
Good fight, Harry. Thanks for the help.

SANBORN
Win a few, lose a few. We'll get 'em next time, young fella.
(moving off)

SLATTERY
Thanks again.

12.

13 FULL SHOT - FEATURING THE ROSTRUM, THE SPEAKER'S STAND AND THE VOTING PANELS

METCAFF
The clerk will close the roll and tally the votes.

The mechanism concealed behind the voting panels goes into action with much CLICK-CLICKING, flashing of numbers in the upper tallying section of the panel and the final vote shows 32 "yes" votes and 39 "no". The identical tallying procedure on the board is repeated three times.

METCAFF
(continuing)
Mister Slattery... what is your pleasure?

Slattery is a bit rueful but responds good-naturedly:

SLATTERY
It's no pleasure, Mister Speaker, but go ahead and announce the vote.

METCAFF
32 "aye"... 39 "no"... the amendments are defeated.

14 CAMERA SHOOTING PAST SLATTERY

seated at his desk, toward Speaker Metcaff presiding at the rostrum.

METCAFF
(continuing)
You will now vote on the bill proper. 41 votes are required for passage. The clerk will prepare the roll.

Again, the soft GONG is heard throughout the chamber to signify that voting is now open. Slattery reaches over, presses the "no" button and CAMERA PANS AROUND so that we see the voting panel as votes are registered. It's quite evident the bill is going to pass. Frank Radcliff moves down the aisle and up beside Slattery.

RADCLIFF
(notes Slattery's expression)
Come off it, Slattery. Our fair state can't be in that much trouble.

(CONTINUED)

14 CONTINUED

SLATTERY
Hi, Frank. What's with you?

RADCLIFF
(hands him press release)
As Minority Leader, I think you ought to find this interesting.

SLATTERY
(looking)
From Elliott's office?

RADCLIFF
I'd like to have your reaction, sir.

Slattery peruses the paper and starts to react almost immediately. In the b.g. we hear:

METCAFF
The clerk will close the roll and tally the votes.

In the b.g. we see and HEAR the voting panel in action as the votes are tallied. The result is 44 "yes" and 28 "no". CAMERA HOLDS on Slattery in the immediate f.g. as he continues to read and react to the contents of the release.

METCAFF
(continuing)
Ayes 44, noes 28. The bill is passed and sent to the Senate.

SLATTERY
(looking up)
Is this for real?

RADCLIFF
(shakes head)
I've been assured by young Senator Elliott himself.

CAMERA PANS SWIFTLY to rostrum where we see Metcaff conferring earnestly in hushed tones with Majority Leader Butler. Metcaff frowns darkly, shakes his head in disgust. Then he turns to the rostrum mike, gavels once.

METCAFF
We have a communication from a member of the Senate. The Clerk will please read.

(CONTINUED)

14.

14 CONTINUED (2):

CAMERA PANS BACK to Slattery and Radcliff.

RADCLIFF
(moves to go)
I'll catch up with you later.

SLATTERY
Okay.

Radcliff exits toward rear of chamber.

15 INT. HOUSE CHAMBER - DAY

CAMERA FEATURING the rostrum, particularly the Speaker's stand. Metcaff reaches over the front of the stand and hands the CHIEF CLERK a two page letter. The Clerk takes it, turns, moves up to his mike and starts to read.

NOTE: Throughout the reading of the letter by the Clerk, CAMERA WILL PICK UP appropriate and meaningful REACTION SHOTS of the following: Slattery, Harry Sanborn, Carl Butler, Senator Bart Elliott, Speaker Metcaff, and Frank Radcliff.

CLERK
Gentlemen: I wish to inform your honorable body that one of your members... with or without the collusion of others ... has deliberately, viciously and with malice aforethought committed a gross violation of the joint rules of this State legislature. The man I accuse is the Chairman of the House Ways and Means Committee... Representative Harry Sanborn.

In a matter of seconds the entire membership is frozen in a deadly silence... perhaps because of surprise, disbelief or the audacity of the charge leveled against such an honored and respected legislator.

CLERK
(continuing)
I charge that Mister Sanborn willfully and illegally killed a Senate bill which had been referred to the House Ways and Means Committee and that he did so without ever giving the full membership of that committee the opportunity to even consider, much less vote on, the bill.
(MORE)

(CONTINUED)

15.

15 CONTINUED

CLERK (cont'd)
The measure I refer to is Senate Bill 209, which I authored and which was passed by a unanimous vote in the upper house. I accuse Representative Harry Sanborn of cold, deliberate and cynical disregard for the joint rules of this legislature and the laws of this state. I am fully aware that these are extraordinary and very serious charges to lodge against an elected official. But I cannot and I will not back down in the face of such outrageous conduct on the part of a member of this legislature. I respectfully ask for a full, impartial and thorough investigation of the charges which I have set down. And I demand that swift and appropriate action be taken against the offending member. Very sincerely yours... Senator Bart Elliott... 18th Senatorial District.

There is a long moment of absolute quiet after the Clerk finishes reading. Then a few scattered, hushed murmurs are heard as Harry Sanborn gets to his feet slowly and raises his mike. He is fighting hard to contain his anger and he's doing a pretty good job at it. He's a real veteran and he shows it. When he speaks, his voice is cold, even, precise.

METCAFF
(noting Sanborn
Mister Sanborn... for what purpose do you rise?

SANBORN
A point of personal privilege, Mister Speaker.

METCAFF
(brief nod)
State your point of personal privilege.

(CONTINUED)

15 CONTINUED - (2):

SANBORN

Mister Speaker... members of the House. If young Senator Elliott felt his bill received unfair treatment in the committee of which I am chairman, why didn't he come to me with his complaints? Or failing that, instead of running first to the press with his accusations why did he not lodge his protests with the presiding officer of the Senate, or the senior members of his party in the Senate? Those are the accepted and traditional channels which honorable legislators have used... at least during my 18 years in this House. Why this sudden hysterical flinging about of sensational charges and lurid accusations? Mister Speaker, I categorically deny his charges and I most certainly welcome a full investigation. In the meantime, so there will be no doubt as to how I view the charges, I wish to step down as Chairman of the House Ways and Means Committee until the truth or falsity of these accusations has been established. Thank you.

Sanborn sits down and there is immediate and much excited talk from the membership. Metcaff gavels once.

METCAFF

I appreciate your feelings, Mister Sanborn, but I must decline your offer to step down as committee chairman. We will discuss this matter in the Speaker's chambers immediately after adjournment today.

CUT TO:

16 INT. CORRIDOR - ROTUNDA

CAMERA FEATURES Senator Elliott being interviewed by a TV NEWS REPORTER before a pair of newsreel cameras. There are a couple of lights and pieces of portable sound and camera equipment strewn down the corridor. The TV Reporter holds a mike in front of Elliott as he speaks. Slattery and Radcliff move up and pause close

(CONTINUED)

17.

16 CONTINUED

to several curious bystanders seen in the background.

ELLIOTT
(as if continuing)
... As for Representative Sanborn's accusation that my charges are politically inspired, nothing could be farther from the truth.

TV REPORTER
Then you are going to press for a full investigation?

ELLIOTT
Most certainly. I will not rest until my charges are substantiated and Harry Sanborn is driven out of state government... which to my mind is no more than he justly deserves.

TV REPORTER
(brief nod)
All right, Senator. Thank you.

CAMERA PANS SWIFTLY DOWN the corridor and HOLDS on Slattery and Frank Radcliff who stand on the edge of the small gathering who have been witnessing the corridor news interview.

RADCLIFF
Sounds like he means it.

SLATTERY
(wry smile)
One of the first rules of politics. No matter what you say... always sound like you mean it.

Slattery turns and makes his way down the corridor, Radcliff looking after him.

17 INT. SPEAKER'S OFFICE - DAY

It is a much more imposing, more impressive, more spacious office than that of the rank-and-file members of the House (such as Slattery's office which we will see later on). Speaker Bert Metcaff is seated behind his desk and Majority Leader Carl Butler is seated in front of and to one side of the desk, as is the Chairman of the

(CONTINUED)

18.

17 CONTINUED

House Rules Committee, WESLEY GIBBONS. Gibbons is in his mid-50's, paunchy, slightly balding. His attitude is brusque, glowering. Harry Sanborn is seated to Gibbons' left.

BUTLER
(turns to Sanborn)
Go ahead, Harry... What's Elliott's bill all about anyway?

SANBORN
(checks notes)
Mainly it provides for the state to acquire ten thousand acres of forest land in my district. The acreage is in the Warm Valley area... about 30 miles north of Kingsburg.

METCAFF
And the land was supposed to be developed into a state park?

SANBORN
(nods)
With full recreational facilities for the general public. The bill also provides that part of the land be developed into a large summer camp for underprivileged kids.

GIBBONS
(grunts)
Leave it to Elliott... that's a sure vote-getter, isn't it?

SANBORN
The bill ran through the Senate without any trouble, then it came over here, got through Natural Resources committee and was sent on to Ways and Means.

BUTLER
And you were opposed to the bill?

(CONTINUED)

19.

17 CONTINUED - (2):

SANBORN
(nods)
Certainly. Not because of the contents. I think there's a legitimate need for a state park like that. But it's a bad deal for my district. You take 10-thousand acres, turn it into a park and our county can't tax the land any more. So how do we make up the tax money that's lost? More taxes on the farmers and the home-owners. I'm not about to buy that. My county's given up enough land to the state and federal government as it is. Let 'em find another site for the park.

METCAFF
I see your point. How'd you handle the bill.

SANBORN
I named a 3-man sub-committee to study the thing further. They came back with a report that recommended <u>against</u> passage of the bill. The report was voted on by the full committee and the bill was killed.

GIBBONS
So the vote's recorded and the bill's dead. What's all the arguing about?

SANBORN
(a bit dourly)
Just one little detail. The committee secretary, Miss Corbin, can't seem to find anything in the notes she took at the meeting to indicate the sub-committee report on Elliott's bill was even discussed... much less voted on.

GIBBONS
You mean there's no written evidence that the bill was voted on by the full committee?

(CONTINUED)

20.

17 CONTINUED - (3):

SANBORN
(bit grimly; shakes head)
We haven't come up with anything so far.

BUTLER
How about the committee members? Any of them recall voting on the report?

SANBORN
You've chaired enough committees, Carl... you know how the routine has to go. The day I'm supposed to have committed the great crime Ways and Means had 36 different bills to consider. We had a 5-hour afternoon session and another session at night that finally wound up at 1:45 A.M.
(brief pause)
Any wonder if a man can't recall all the details of a session like that?

METCAFF
(grunts)
None at all.
(rises; starting to pace room)
Harry, we've been up here a long time. We know how mistakes can happen. But how can we possibly explain to the public that a piece of legislation was destroyed by a simple "clerical" error?

Metcaff lights a cigarette.

SANBORN
(quietly)
Get to the point, Bert.

METCAFF
(candidly)
Elliott's got us backed into a corner. This is one time we can't afford to duck.

SANBORN
For the good of the party.

METCAFF
That's right.

(CONTINUED)

21.

17 CONTINUED - (4):

SANBORN
(brief sigh; wearily)
The dear old party.

METCAFF
I can't see any other way out.
There's got to be an investigation.

Sanborn gets to his feet.

SANBORN
Okay, Bert... you're calling the
shots. Turn the bloodhounds
loose.

CUT TO:

18 INT. SLATTERY'S OFFICE - NIGHT - BIG CLOSE SHOT -
SLATTERY

He's contentious, indignant, his voice raised. CAMERA
PULLS BACK during the ensuing dialogue.

SLATTERY
(vehemently)
Why not? Why not? You ask me
to head up this investigation
knowing full well that Harry
Sanborn's one of the best friends
I own?

METCAFF
(clipped, forceful)
You're the House Minority Leader.
Do you make legislative decisions
on the basis of friendship?

SLATTERY
(unmoved)
You still haven't come in
from left field, Bert. The
newspapermen up here don't
walk around with blinders on.
I know exactly the kind of
stories they'll be filing out
of here. "Sanborn's close friend
to conduct investigation of
Sanborn..."

(CONTINUED)

22.

18 CONTINUED

METCAFF
(shakes head)
The newsmen up here put the mark on you a long time ago, Slattery. You're square and you're a hard-head and you've burned us up plenty of times. But I can't think of anyone less likely to be swayed by friendship or anything else when it comes to doing your job in the House.

SLATTERY
(sharply)
My job? Now that's an interesting point. Who's involved in this mess anyway? Bart Elliott... the Senate brass... yourself... Wes Gibbons... Carl Butler... Harry Sanborn... all members of the majority party.

METCAFF
This thing involves a lot more than party politics, can't you see that? When Elliott made those charges, he wasn't just taking on Harry Sanborn... he was taking on the entire House. He's questioning the honesty of our committee system... he's challenging our whole operation. Besides, you claim you're worried that Sanborn's going to get a smear job... you wonder how the investigating committee's going to treat him. Well, what better way to make sure that he does get a fair, honest shake than if you're heading up the committee?
(brief pause)
You'll be doing Harry a real favor. Fact is, you'll be doing all of us a favor.

There is a long pause as Slattery paces the room, turns and fixes Metcaff with an almost angry glare.

(CONTINUED)

23.

18 CONTINUED (2):

SLATTERY
(coldly, candidly)
Let's get one thing straight, Bert. If I'm running the show, the investigation's going to be done my way. We're going to dig all the way to the bottom and I don't care how many skeletons we find. And if I happen to tromp on the toes of half the brass in the majority party, well, too bad... you asked for it. All right?

Metcaff nods somberly as he gets to his feet.

METCAFF
(rising)
I promised you a free hand... you've got it.
(moving to door)
Make it move, Slattery. The longer this thing hangs the more flies it's going to draw.
(stops, turns)
Get it done as fast as you possibly can.

Metcaff EXITS, Slattery looking after him, frowning thoughtfully.

DISSOLVE:

19 INT. SLATTERY'S OUTER OFFICE - NIGHT

Slattery crosses over to get his hat and coat which are hanging on a stand. Slattery's secretary, LIZ, an attractive woman, mature, competent, is busy closing up.

SLATTERY
(as he gets hat and coat)
So, I'm a prize sucker to take that committee chairmanship... is that what you mean?

(CONTINUED)

19 CONTINUED

LIZ
I have labored in the political jungles for 14 years, Mister Slattery. I think I know the terrain very well. But I can't assist you and I can't offer advice until you take me into your confidence... before you make decisions.

SLATTERY
(off-handedly)
Sorry, Liz... it won't happen again.

By now, Liz has arisen, slipped into her coat and is pulling her gloves on. She is pleasantly annoyed but not angry.

LIZ
Oh, yes it will... again and again, and again. But I would like to remind you that I am an administrative assistant. And occasionally I do indeed enjoy the feeling that I'm earning my keep and that I am indeed doing the job I was hired to do. That's all, Mister Slattery, sir. End of complaint.

During the last few lines of her speech, Liz crosses from behind her desk, moves to the door and holds it open. Slattery grins, exits, Liz following.

20 INT. CORRIDOR - NIGHT

The corridor is fairly deserted. CAMERA LEADS Slattery and Liz as they make their way down the corridor.

SLATTERY
So give me some expert opinion. Where's the main support coming from for Senator Elliott's famous bill?

Liz's response is immediate... at the fingertips. She's highly efficient but not officious.

LIZ
The big push is coming from youth organizations... the outdoorsy folk... the posy-pickers. Alan Morrow, the parks
(MORE)

(CONTINUED)

20 CONTINUED

LIZ (cont'd)
director, is working hard for it, too.

SLATTERY
Oh? Did you follow the bill at all?

LIZ
I heard Senator Elliott and Mister Sanborn argue it out when it came before Natural Resources Committee. Sanborn's main concern seems to be the Warm Valley area. I guess that's where his county gets most of its tax revenue.

Slattery grunts thoughtfully. They reach a turn in the corridor and Liz starts to move off.

LIZ
(continuing)
Now if you'll excuse me, sir. I'm going out for refueling.

SLATTERY
I've got Johnny holding a table down at Wing's... why don't you join us?

LIZ
(slight, sly grin)
I'm sorry, sir, but you and your devoted legislative intern will have to do without sparkling little me for this evening.

SLATTERY
Got a date?

LIZ
(slight nod)
A rather handsome old party from Agriculture Department. Named Amos Michael Thursby. A lovely dancer.

(CONTINUED)

26.

20 CONTINUED - (2):

SLATTERY
Oh?

LIZ
Indeed. He's a marvelous conversationalist, too, but he seems to be limited strictly to one subject: "The Ethiopian hybrid kumquat... its planting and care."
(grins, turns)
Goodnight, Sir Boss.

She turns and moves off. Slattery grins and starts off in the opposite direction.

CUT TO:

21 EXT. STATE CAPITOL - NIGHT

CAMERA FEATURES Slattery's lone figure as he exits the building, makes his way wearily down the steps and starts down the walk bordering the curved driveway leading to the street.

22 ANOTHER ANGLE - SLATTERY

A car, moving in the same direction as Slattery, overtakes him and pulls to a stop. The driver is PAT RUSSELL... tall, leggy, and as bright as she is beautiful.

PAT
Taxi, Mister Slattery?

SLATTERY
'Evening, lady. Would you happen to be going by that famous Chinese beanery?

PAT
I might. Climb in and take a chance.

Slattery opens the door, gets in and the car moves slowly down the driveway to the street.

23 INT. PAT RUSSELL'S CAR - NIGHT

Throughout the ensuing dialogue, Slattery takes out a pack of cigarettes, lights one and hands it to Pat, then lights another for himself.

SLATTERY
Working pretty late, aren't you, Pat?

PAT
(nodding)
The executive branch of government has its problems, too.

SLATTERY
(grunts)
Not too surprising... when you consider the incumbent executive.

Pat tosses him a scolding grin as she pulls up for an arterial stop.

PAT
Snide fellow. Shall I drop you here?

SLATTERY
(grins)
You're getting sensitive. How is the dear old governor?

Pat presses the accelerator, the car moves forward.

PAT
Very well and very busy.

SLATTERY
What's he doing about those three bills of mine sitting on his desk?

PAT
They're still sitting there. Awaiting signature.

SLATTERY
Miss Russell... could I possibly persuade you to say a few words to the governor about those bills?

(CONTINUED)

28

23 CONTINUED

PAT
You could not.

SLATTERY
Just a few kind words. I'd appreciate it, Pat.

PAT
(but curtly)
When you talk like that I get the distinct impression this friendship exists only because you're trying to use me.

SLATTERY
You're absolutely right. I am.

Pat glances at him briefly, grins tolerantly.

SLATTERY
(continuing)
After all, what are friends for?

PAT
You're ambivalent, Slattery.
(pointedly, glancing at him)
You presented quite a different case last weekend.

SLATTERY
(grins)
Touché.
(reflecting, quietly)
It was fun.

PAT
Uh-huh. Beautiful night. And you didn't mention politics once.

SLATTERY
My big weakness. I can only concentrate on one thing at a time.

29.

24 EXT. STREET - NIGHT

Pat's car turns the corner coming TOWARD CAMERA which PANS with the car as it swings into a parking lot immediately adjoining Wing Fong's restaurant and comes to a stop. A neon sign much in evidence in the b.g. proclaims: WING FONG'S - CHINESE-AMERICAN FOOD.

25 INT. PAT'S CAR - NIGHT

as Slattery moves as if to exit. Pat lays a restraining hand on his arm.

PAT
Slattery...

He pauses.

PAT
(continuing)
I'll make it short. There are two people in this town I'm very fond of and one of them's Harry Sanborn.

SLATTERY
You got the word?

PAT
(nodding)
This is slightly confidential, but last week I heard the governor is thinking seriously of appointing Harry Sanborn to fill the vacancy on the State Supreme Court.

SLATTERY
(quiet surprise)
Oh?

PAT
I'm not sure what effect the investigation's going to have on his chances now. I just wanted you to know what the situation is.

(CONTINUED)

30.

25 CONTINUED

SLATTERY
(grunts, frowns)
Thanks.
(turning to her)
Y'know, this whole mess seems to stem from a lack of coordination among your troops in the majority party. I hear that Alan Morrow, your governor's Director of Parks, was very busy pushing for the bill that got Harry Sanborn into this trouble ... correct?

PAT
(brief shrug)
The governor's entitled to a few mistakes. Alan Morrow's example number one. Incidentally, if you have any dealings with him, I suggest you watch what you say. His department has a cute habit of bugging phone conversations.

SLATTERY
Thanks... I'll keep that in mind.
(pats her arm)
Well, good night, lady. Dinner next week?

She nods. There is no embrace, only a brief, meaningful exchange of glances... which say everything that needs to be said.

PAT
Good night.

He exits car and Pat drives off. He turns and starts for the main entrance to Wing Fong's.

26 INT. WING FONG'S RESTAURANT - NIGHT

The interior decor and dressing is an odd mixture of "old" and "new" Chinese. The place is jammed with legislators, lobbyists and various state officials, major and minor. CAMERA FEATURES Slattery as he edges his way through the foyer, past the bar and back into the restaurant proper. As he edges through the crowd, nodding or exchanging an occasional "hello" with an acquaintance, he suddenly spots someone of interest o.s. He heads in that direction.

27 INT. WING FONG'S DINING ROOM - NIGHT

CAMERA FEATURING Harry Sanborn as he waves goodbye to a table-hopper and spots Slattery moving up to his booth. Sanborn is relaxed, his usual congenial self. There's a cup of coffee on the table in front of him and it's apparent he's already had dinner.

SLATTERY
Hi, Harry.

SANBORN
(cheerfully)
And a good evening to you, Mister Minority Leader.
(gesturing)
Come in out of the storm. Sit down.

SLATTERY
(sitting)
Where's Mary? I heard she was coming up for the weekend.

SANBORN
She's here...
(glancing across the crowded room)
... over table-hopping with Buzz Granville and his wife.
(checks watch)
And if we're going to make that show out at the Red Barn she'd better cut it short.

SLATTERY
Harry, I guess you heard about my committee appointment.

SANBORN
I did.

There's just a touch of uneasiness about Slattery's manner.

SLATTERY
(soberly, directly)
I wanted to take a fast reading ... I mean it's kind of an awkward deal... I'd like to make sure there's no misunderstanding.

(CONTINUED)

32.

27 CONTINUED

SANBORN
C'mon, young fella, we know each other better than that. You've been given a job to do, so go ahead and do it.
(a bit pointedly)
And I hope you know what I mean by that.

SLATTERY
I think so.

SANBORN
Don't do me any favors. Play it straight down the middle... all the way.
(sudden grin)
Not that you'd be likely to play it any other way.

SLATTERY
Tell me one thing, Harry... that secretary who covered Ways and Means Committee... has she been able to find any pertinent notes at all on the handling of Elliott's bill? I mean when it came back from sub-committee?

SANBORN
(shaking head)
I've had the files turned upside down.

SLATTERY
(grunts, frowns)
The thing that really bugs me is that if the sub-committee report on Elliott's bill wasn't presented to the full committee for a vote, then how come an entry was made in the official committee records?

SANBORN
Don't you think it bugs me, too? I've seen clerical mistakes happen up here... plenty of them... but I've never come across one like this.

MARY (o.s.)
Don't bother with introductions, Harry...

28 ANOTHER ANGLE

to include MARY SANBORN, who has just moved up beside the booth. She's smiling, pleasant-looking, a motherly type in her mid-50's. She exhibits a quiet, subdued, genuine warmth... nothing effusive about her.

MARY
(continuing)
I believe I know this young man.

Slattery is immediately on his feet and he and Mary embrace briefly, Slattery kissing her on the cheek.

SLATTERY
(as he moves)
Mary... how are you... real good to see you.

MARY
Good to see you, Slattery.

SANBORN
Excuse me, madam, but if we're going to see that show we've got to be moving.
(to Slattery)
Keep her nailed down, will you? I'll have Wing get us a cab.

Sanborn moves off toward the front of the restaurant. Slattery turns back to Mary.

SLATTERY
So c'mon... I haven't seen you in months. What's new down your way?

MARY
I'm a grandma again, that's what's new.

SLATTERY
Congratulations. Which one of 'em did it this time?

MARY
I'm glad to say it was Linda. She's the only daughter that happens to be married.

SLATTERY
I keep forgetting. How about Tod and Evelyn?

(CONTINUED)

34.

28 CONTINUED

MARY
Tod graduates this fall...
Evelyn's still doing post-grad
work. Enough of that... what've
you been up to?

SLATTERY
The usual. Bugging the opposition,
including your husband.

MARY
(candidly)
And how's the love life?

SLATTERY
(slight shrug)
Same.

MARY
There must be something worth
talking about.

SLATTERY
Uh-huh, but it's none of your
business. You're getting to be
a nosey old harridan.

MARY
None of my business? Who
introduced you to that girl in
the first place?

SANBORN (o.s.)
(over the babble
of the crowd)
Mary?... C'mon... the cab's
waiting.

Mary notes his call, waves that she is coming, turns back to Slattery.

MARY
I have to run...
(reaches up,
kisses him on
the cheek)
I don't know how you manage it.

SLATTERY
What?

MARY
Staying single.
(moving off)
Good night, young fella. See
you tomorrow maybe.

(CONTINUED)

35.

28 CONTINUED - (2):

SLATTERY
Good night.

Slattery watches her leave for a moment, then turns and makes his way toward the back of the restaurant.

29 INT. WING FONG'S - NIGHT

As Slattery starts up the stairs to the upper floor he turns and calls back to the bartender.

SLATTERY
Cecil? Send me up a scotch and water, will you please?

30 ANOTHER ANGLE - THE STAIRCASE

As Slattery turns and resumes climbing the stairs to the upper floor he almost collides with Johnny Ramos and a very attractive young GIRL who are standing and chatting intimately a few steps up from the main floor.

JOHNNY
Oh, hi, Mister Slattery. I was just about to go looking for you.

Amused, Slattery glances at Johnny, then at the girl.

SLATTERY
Oh?
(looks back at Johnny)
Why?

JOHNNY
(bit confused)
Well...

He turns to the girl, pats her gently on the upper arm.

JOHNNY
(continuing)
Sure nice seeing you again, Fannie. I'll give you a call in the morning... good night.

The girl nods and exits down the narrow staircase, Slattery and Johnny looking after her.

(CONTINUED)

36

30 CONTINUED

JOHNNY
(continuing; half apologetic)
An old friend from college days.
Fannie.

SLATTERY
(nods: a statement)
Fannie.

JOHNNY
Uh-huh. Sorry I didn't introduce the two of you... I couldn't remember her last name.
(weak snicker)
Kind of embarrassing, y'know?

Slattery grins, delivers a couple of fatherly slaps to Johnny's shoulder.

SLATTERY
Forget it, John. For a legislative intern I'd say you're doing pretty well. Besides...
(nods toward base of stairs)
... with endowments like that who's interested in last names.

JOHNNY
(hastily)
Ah... you want to come on up? I've got a table saved for us.

SLATTERY
Lead on.

They start up the stairs, CAMERA LEADING them.

SLATTERY
(continuing)
John... Liz tells me that State Parks Division is one of the groups backing Senator Elliott's bill... that the way you hear it?

JOHNNY
I don't know about the whole division but the head man over there is sure backing it. Mister Alan Morrow.

(CONTINUED)

30 CONTINUED - (2):

SLATTERY
Then I want you to call his office first thing in the morning. Tell 'em I want a meeting with Mister Morrow right after lunch. In my office.

DISSOLVE:

31 INT. SLATTERY'S OFFICE - DAY - MED. CLOSE SHOT - STATE DIRECTOR OF PARKS, ALAN MORROW

MORROW is in his late forties, well-fed, overly ingratiating and apparently perpetually insecure. His inferiors, his departmental staff, he treats high-handedly. He wants them to regard him in a godly light. To his equals or superiors, on the other hand, he wishes to be regarded as a cheerful always helpful, dedicated public servant. Above all he wants to avoid trouble of any kind.

During the ensuing dialogue CAMERA PULLS BACK to reveal the rest of the room and Slattery seated behind his desk. Slattery is snappy, all business, as he consults a sheaf of papers on the desk in front of him.

SLATTERY
You supported Senator Elliott's bill, didn't you, Mister Morrow?

MORROW
Well, of course I'm not a member of the legislature... I took no official position...

SLATTERY
Were you aware from the very beginning that Mister Sanborn was against it? That he was bitterly opposed to it?

(CONTINUED)

38.

31 CONTINUED

MORROW
Well, yes, I was. But it's not that I blame him, mind you. After all, his county would lose 10 thousand acres of taxable land. That wouldn't please his constituents very much.

SLATTERY
It's my understanding that Mister Sanborn was concerned mainly with the north portion of the 10 thousand acres... the section called Warm Valley.

MORROW
Yes. I recall him mentioning that during the hearings.

SLATTERY
What's your opinion, Mister Morrow... do you think it was a clerical mistake or did Sanborn kill that bill deliberately?

MORROW
Please, Mister Slattery. I'm in no position to answer that. This is a matter for the legislature... I don't want to get involved.

SLATTERY
Did Sanborn ever talk to you about the bill?

MORROW
(brief pause)
Yes.

SLATTERY
And?

MORROW
He said he was opposed to it. He tried to swing me around to his way of thinking.

(CONTINUED)

39.

31 CONTINUED: - (2)

SLATTERY
Was anyone else present when you had that conversation?

MORROW
No, I don't believe so.

SLATTERY
(rising)
Mister Morrow, did Harry Sanborn ever pressure you to use your influence to change the location of the proposed park?

MORROW
No.

SLATTERY
Did anyone ever pressure you to go one way or another on the bill?

MORROW
This whole thing's a matter for the legislature. It's none of my business.

SLATTERY
It _is_ your business, Morrow. Do you know of any reason, any motivation that would prompt any pressure group to try and block the establishment of this park area?

Morrow gets to his feet a bit shakily.

MORROW
Mister Slattery, I'm not involved in this fight and I don't intend to become involved. Now if you'll excuse me...
(starting for door)

SLATTERY
Morrow...

Morrow exits.

32 INT. SLATTERY'S OUTER OFFICE - DAY

Liz is seated behind her desk, looks at the door closing in the wake of Morrow's departure. Slattery enters the shot, moves up to the desk and takes a message memo proferred him by Liz.

LIZ
(handing him memo)
The Speaker's office called. Both of your nominees for the investigating committee were accepted without question.

SLATTERY
(looking at message)
Stan Wills... John Underwood. Good.

LIZ
Shall I call the gentlemen and set the first meeting for tomorrow?

Slattery crumples the phone message and tosses it into the wastebasket

SLATTERY
Better put it off a couple of days.

LIZ
(reacting)
Oh?

SLATTERY
Tomorrow I'm driving down to Orchard County... Harry Sanborn's district. If anyone asks, I'm away on legislative business.
(rising)
And line up another car for Johnny, will you? I want him to meet me down there.

LIZ
Indeed. And do I dare inquire the reason for all this?

SLATTERY
Mister Morrow is a very disturbed civil servant. I'd like to find out why.

DISSOLVE:

41.

33 EXT. COUNTY COURTHOUSE PARKING LOT - DAY

CAMERA FEATURING Johnny as he drives his car into the courthouse parking lot. He spots a familiar car just inside the driveway and stops beside it. We see Slattery exit from the second car, cross over and get into Johnny's car.

34 INT. CAR - DAY - TWO SHOT - JOHNNY AND SLATTERY

as the latter enters.

JOHNNY
Have you been waiting long?

SLATTERY
(shakes head)
Couple of minutes. Make a right turn as you come out of the driveway, huh? We're heading north.

JOHNNY
Yes sir.

The car starts to move.

DISSOLVE:

35 INT. CAR - DAY

The car is traveling through mountain country. Johnny is driving.

SLATTERY
So fill me in. How did you make out over in Reddington?

JOHNNY
I tagged all the bases but I don't know what I've got to show for it.

SLATTERY
Give me a sample.

JOHNNY
(frowns thoughtfully)
Seems like Mr. Sanborn's got the support of a good 90 per cent of the people. Businessmen and the Chamber of Commerce like him... so do the labor groups, church and women's
(MORE)

(CONTINUED)

42.

35 CONTINUED

JOHNNY (cont'd)
clubs, the farmers, teachers' associations, the city council, the mayor, couple of judges... they think he's the greatest.

SLATTERY
And the state park deal? How do they feel about that?

JOHNNY
They're backing Sanborn a hundred percent. As far as Warm Valley goes, apparently nobody has any interest in the area. No plans for commercial or industrial development of any kind.

Slattery grunts, stares ahead thoughtfully.

JOHNNY (cont'd)
That's about it. How'd you make out in Kingsburg?

SLATTERY
Like you did in Reddington... Harry Sanborn's the greatest... nobody wants to lose the Warm Valley acreage... but no one has any personal interest in it either.

JOHNNY
I guess that does it.

SLATTERY
Not quite. Long as we're in the neighborhood we might as well take a look at Warm Valley firsthand. Talk to some of the folks up there.

JOHNNY
Anything special in mind?

SLATTERY
There's only one way to run an investigation, John boy. Ask questions.

36 EXT. MOUNTAIN COUNTRY ROAD - DAY

CAMERA FEATURING the car as it travels along a two lane road.

DISSOLVE:

43.

37 EXT. SHOULDER OF MOUNTAIN ROAD - DAY

CAMERA FEATURES Slattery and Johnny talking with a fisherman, HERMAN, who is gesturing in the direction of the nearby slopes leading down to a river.

HERMAN
There were about six or eight fellas, all told. I saw them working there on the slopes... either side of the river. They had some kind of equipment with 'em and they went up and down the slopes digging holes in the ground. Got no idea what they were up to.

SLATTERY
You mind pointing out exactly where they were working?

HERMAN
Not 'tall.
(indicating)
First time I saw 'em they were right along there...

SLATTERY
(turns to leave)
Thank you, sir. Much obliged.

HERMAN
Don't mention it.

CUT TO

38 EXT. RIVER BANK - DAY - CLOSE SHOT - GROUND

where a fairly recent "core drilling" has been made. Slattery's hand comes into the picture, he picks up a piece of earth which has been pressed into a cylindrical shape. CAMERA PULLS BACK to HOLD on Slattery and Johnny in a TIGHT TWO SHOT as they examine the piece of earth, reacting.

SLATTERY
Somebody's been doing some core drilling.

JOHNNY
I'm a city boy myself. Why would they do that?

SLATTERY
To get specimens of soil and rock formations from below the surface.

(CONTINUED)

44.

38 CONTINUED

JOHNNY
Some kind of a mining deal?

SLATTERY
I don't know.

Slattery tosses the piece of soil away, gets to his feet from his stooped position.

SLATTERY
(continuing)
Let's head back for Kingsburg, John. I've got some more questions to ask.

DISSOLVE:

39 INT. SANBORN'S APARTMENT - NIGHT

It is neatly but not expensively furnished. CLOSE SHOT of Sanborn who is seated in a chair with a drink in his hand. During ensuing dialogue, CAMERA PULLS BACK to reveal Slattery sitting opposite Sanborn. He, too, has a drink.

SANBORN
Sorry, young fella. You made the trip for nothing.

SLATTERY
(quietly)
No I didn't. I'm going to get what I came for.

There is a pause. Sanborn nods to indicate.

SANBORN
Drink your Scotch.

SLATTERY
I've been put off long enough. It's getting late... I need some answers.

SANBORN
(flaring up)
All right, so what do you want from me? Shall I stand up and swear I'm innocent? Privately? To you? Off-the-record?

(CONTINUED)

45.

39 CONTINUED

SLATTERY
I only want to know two things...
Number one, did you ever pressure
Alan Morrow about Elliott's bill?

SANBORN
What do you mean, 'pressure'?
I called him a couple of times
and told him how I felt about
the bill. Period.

SLATTERY
Then tell me this: what do
you know about a survey team
working down in Warm Valley a
couple of weeks ago? They made
at least a dozen core-drillings
up and down the slopes.

SANBORN
Why should I know anything about
a survey team in Warm Valley?

SLATTERY
Because it's in your district.
And you know everything that
goes on in your district.

SANBORN
(irked)
If you're curious why don't you
check with the County Departments
in Kingsburg?

SLATTERY
I did. They clammed up. No
one knew anything about anything.

SANBORN
Then why come to me? I've got
enough work to keep me tied to
my desk right here.

SLATTERY
(coldly, steadily)
Make it yes or no, that's all
I'm asking. Do you know anything
about those core-drillings?

(CONTINUED)

46.

39 CONTINUED - (2):

SANBORN
(after a pause;
quietly)
Slattery... do you feel you owe me anything?

SLATTERY
(evenly)
I'd give you both arms if you asked me.

SANBORN
All I'm asking for is your trust. A little faith. I ask you to believe that in all my years in the House I have done my job honestly. I've played rough. But I've always played square. And I have always represented my district. My people... rich or poor, it's never made any difference to me.

SLATTERY
And what about the rest of the people of the State? Don't they rate in your book?

SANBORN
I'm not elected by the people of this state. I'm elected by the people of the 21st District. My first concern is for them.

SLATTERY
I don't know what you're getting at, Harry, but it sounds like you're copping a plea.

SANBORN
You can read it any way you like.

SLATTERY
You're not going to answer my question, is that final?

SANBORN
(flares up)
It's absolutely final so don't ask me again.

Slattery gets to his feet.

(CONTINUED)

47.

39 CONTINUED - (3):

SLATTERY
Then I'm going to call you back before the committee. And I'm going to ask you the same question.

Sanborn reacts, quietly, coldly.

SANBORN
Politics has been my whole life. And I have a strong sense of self-survival. But if I'm forced to go, I want you to realize... I'll do everything in my power to take you with me.

Slattery stands there motionless for a moment reacting... stunned, disappointed but still determined.

SLATTERY
(curt nod)
G'night, Harry.

Slattery exits.

DISSOLVE:

40 INT. COMMITTEE MEETING ROOM - DAY

It's a comparatively small chamber if you're speaking in terms of the average committee meeting room but it's entirely adequate for a committee of this size. There is no room for spectators and there are no spectators. Those present include Slattery, Liz (who as committee-secretary is taking note of the proceedings), the other two members of the committee, Representatives STANLEY WILLS (Majority Party), and JOHN UNDERWOOD (Minority Party). They are grouped around one end of a conference table. The chair at the opposite end of the table is for the various witnesses who appear to testify before the committee. Scene opens with a MED. CLOSE PROFILE SHOT of Stanley Wills in the immediate f.g.

WILLS
(irate)
...But we've heard all the testimony from the people involved... why prolong this thing?

SLATTERY
Because I want to recall a witness.

(CONTINUED)

40 CONTINUED

WILLS
Who?

SLATTERY
Harry Sanborn.

UNDERWOOD
But he's already appeared once.
It's not very pleasant to sit
in that chair down there and
defend yourself repeatedly...

SLATTERY
I'm chairman of the committee,
Mister Wills. That gives me the
privilege of calling the shots.
I want the witness recalled.

UNDERWOOD
I have to take exception... I
don't think you're being fair...

Slattery tosses a small book abruptly on the desk in front of Underwood.

SLATTERY
(snaps angrily)
There's the book of rules, John.
Show me where it says I have to
be fair.

There is cold silence in the room for a moment, then Underwood and Wills get to their feet, pick up their portfolios and turn to leave.

UNDERWOOD
All right, Mister Chairman. Have
it your way.

Wills and Underwood exit. Liz starts to collect her papers, glances coldly at Slattery.

LIZ
And just how long do you intend
keeping your little secret?

SLATTERY
Until I find out how it relates
to this case. All I know is a
survey team was working down in
Warm Valley. Who they are and
why they were there I have no
idea. And I'm not about to pop
off until Harry Sanborn decides
to talk to me about it.

(CONTINUED)

40 CONTINUED - (2):

LIZ
Excuse the admonition, but you don't have the right to withhold information from committee members.

SLATTERY
(irked)
Now just a minute...

LIZ
(breaks in)
No sir... I beg your pardon all over the place, Mister Slattery, but so far you've been doing a one-man show. Wills and Underwood don't count in your book. You're running a <u>one-man committee.</u>
(brief pause)
And that's the very same thing Harry Sanborn's accused of doing ... isn't it!

She turns and exits.

41 INT. CAPITOL CORRIDOR - DAY

The offices which open on to this particular section of the corridor are occupied by members of the press, television and radio. Signs jutting out over each of the doors indicate the occupant's affiliation, such as: DAILY NEWS... THE TRIBUNE... TELEVISION NEWS CORP.... and, more pertinently... THE TIMES-CHRONICLE. It is the latter the CAMERA FEATURES in the f.g. as we see Slattery exit the committee room which is directly opposite the TIMES-CHRON office.

RADCLIFF (o.s.)
Slattery?...

Slattery retraces a step or two, pauses at the threshold.

42 INT. RADCLIFF'S OFFICE - NIGHT

It is small, cluttered. Furnishings are what you might expect... desk, typewriter, filing cabinets and a teletype machine.

SLATTERY
Frank... how are you?

(CONTINUED)

50.

42 CONTINUED

RADCLIFF
(rising, crossing
over)
I'm curious, that's how I am.
What's your committee come up
with and when are you going to
release it...?

SLATTERY
(shrugs)
We've heard all the witnesses...
we'll re-examine the testimony
in the next day or so. There's
nothing for release right now.

RADCLIFF
(bit brusquely)
When will there be something?

SLATTERY
(clipped)
We'll re-examine the testimony
and we'll submit our report to
the House when we're good and
ready. Okay?

RADCLIFF
Don't hand me that noise,
Slattery. I've been around this
game too long. You've heard all
the witnesses... It's time to
produce. Either play or get off
the field.

SLATTERY
(quiet anger)
Who the hell do you think you
are to make these demands on me?
Are you the voice of the people
or something? The big watchdog
of the legislature?

RADCLIFF
You just bet your sweet backside
I am, Mister. That's been my
job for 23 years... I'm here to
report what you're doing... what
you're saying, and, yeah, sometimes what you're thinking.

SLATTERY
You better ease off, Frank.
You're getting a Messiah complex.

(CONTINUED)

42 CONTINUED - (2):

RADCLIFF
We've all got complexes, Mister Slattery. Good and bad.

SLATTERY
You trying to make a point?

RADCLIFF
I remember when you first showed up in this town 8 years ago. You had all the polish of a clod-buster and you knew as much about politics as a part-time dog-catcher. I've seen you guys come and go. All of you... honest and crooked... bright and not so bright. I rate you in the bright class, but you've still got a long way to go, Buddy. So don't get hard with your elders and don't turn down a piece of advice I think you can use.

SLATTERY
Advice. We get that by the tonful every day.

RADCLIFF
You can take it or leave it, fella, but I'm warning you: don't play games with this investigation. Get it off the line and wrap it up fast, or believe me, you'll regret it.

Slattery exits, CAMERA HOLDING on Radcliff.

DISSOLVE:

43 EXT. GLORY HOTEL SKYROOM TERRACE - NIGHT

CAMERA HOLDS CLOSE on Pat Russell who stands at the terrace railing with a drink in her hand looking out over the city. She wears a light, bright summer dress and it's obvious she didn't pick up this little number at a neighborhood dress shop. This breezy piece of merchandise (which Pat wears quite casually) is the best that Saks, Magnin's, Bergdorf's, et al had to offer. She is on her third drink and while she isn't feeling much pain, she does not display any obvious signs of being high.

(CONTINUED)

52.

43 CONTINUED

To begin with, her mood is pensive... it seems to warn that something is up and that caution is inorder. This is Slattery's first reaction as he exits the main lounge room in the b.g. with a drink in his hand and crosses to her. His apology is automatic... he's been late for dates with her a dozen times before.

SLATTERY
(moving up beside her)
Sorry I'm late.

She doesn't turn to look at him... continues to gaze out over the city. Her tone is casual, indifferent.

PAT
Don't be. I enjoyed the wait ... for a change. Nice up here this time of night.

Slattery glances at her, senses she's in a mood. He sips his drink.

SLATTERY
(after a pause)
You want another drink?

PAT
(shakes head)
This'll do for now.
(sips drink)

Slattery glances out over the city, then eyes Pat appraisingly.

SLATTERY
About ready for something to eat?

PAT
No rush.

SLATTERY
(after a pause)
What <u>are</u> you ready for?

Pat tenses a bit, sets her glass down, turns and eyes him directly. Her tone is sober, deliberate.

PAT
Slattery... will you please kiss me?

He reacts with mild surprise.

(CONTINUED)

53.

43 CONTINUED - (2):

PAT
(continuing)
I mean it. Kiss me right now. Because we're about to have a terrible argument. And you might never want to kiss me again.

SLATTERY
(moving closer)
I can't think of a better way to start an argument.

He kisses her and it's a long lingering embrace, because Pat wants it that way. Finally they break. Pat's voice is a husky whisper.

PAT
(solemnly)
I've never asked you for anything before. But I'm asking you now.

SLATTERY
(brief pause)
Go ahead... ask.

PAT
I admit I'm interfering. I know it's none of my business. But I want you to resign as committee chairman. Tonight.. tomorrow... as soon as possible.

Slattery reacts. She has just stepped on to very shaky ground... into a corner of his life where she doesn't belong, and she knows it as well as he.

SLATTERY
(crisply)
I'll buy the first half of that, lady. You are interfering. It's none of your business.

PAT
I'm not exactly a stranger to you. That gives me some right to speak up.

SLATTERY
(coldly)
Tell me more.

(CONTINUED)

43 CONTINUED - (3):

PAT
(reacts)
Take that tone with me just once more and so help me I'll slap you silly. Maybe you don't realize it but I'm talking sense. You don't build a political career by playing a hatchet-man.

SLATTERY
Is that how you rate me?

PAT
That's how a lot of people around here rate you these days. And that includes Harry Sanborn. He's been hurt, Slattery. Personally and politically. And you're going to be hurt, too, if you keep on.

SLATTERY
When I took this job I promised everybody concerned they'd get a cold, impartial, honest shake. And that's exactly what they're getting... Harry Sanborn included.

PAT
You know something? You're beginning to sound like a member of the Wreck-Harry-Sanborn Club. Like Alan Morrow for instance.

SLATTERY
You're drunk.

PAT
(angrily)
Drunk or sober... get out of this thing. It isn't your problem. Get out now!

Slattery eyes her for a long moment... then he asks quietly:

SLATTERY
Tell me something, lady. Who put you up to this? Was it the Governor? Or the Speaker? Or was it Mister Sanborn?

(CONTINUED)

55.

43 CONTINUED - (4):

Obviously... judging from Pat's reaction... he could not have asked a more insulting question. She comes up with a wicked right and lands a solid, stinging back-hand slap across his face. Then she turns and stalks off, while Slattery watches her expressionlessly. He looks down at his drink, raises his glass and empties it. Then he sets the glass down and starts for the open sliding glass door which leads to the main lounge inside.

44 REVERSE ANGLE

CAMERA SHOOTING OUT toward the terrace as Slattery enters the room from the terrace and moves over to a telephone stand a few steps to one side of the door. He takes a small black book from his pocket, and flips through the pages until he finds the number he wants. Then he picks up the receiver, inserts a coin and dials.

SLATTERY
Mister Alan Morrow, please.
(after a pause)
Morrow, this is Slattery. We've got to have a talk. Tonight... You can't or you won't?... Then in that case we'll be handing out subpoenas in the morning... where do you want yours delivered? Uh-huh. Thanks, I appreciate it. I'll meet you in half an hour. No. This time we'll make it in <u>your</u> office.

He hangs up and exits.

DISSOLVE:

45 INSERT - TELETYPE MACHINE

We hear 5 bells SOUND and the machine then rapidly spells out the following:

(CONTINUED)

56.

45 CONTINUED

TIMES-CHRON DESK

FYI - SLATTERY COMMITTEE

REPORT SPECIAL ORDER OF HOUSE

3:30 P. WILL PRESENT

WITNESS BEFORE REPORT.

EXPECT BULLETIN LEAD

FOR NINE-STAR.

RADCLIFF - CAPITOL

CUT TO:

46 INT. THE HOUSE CHAMBER - DAY

CAMERA SHOOTING DOWN on a FULL SHOT of the House floor. It's a few minutes before the membership convenes and there is much tension and excitement in the air which is reflected mostly by the nervous activity of the clerical staff members up on the lower rostrum as they prepare for the opening of the legislative day.

A special table for the use of Slattery's committee has been set up below and directly in front of the rostrum. There are four microphones on the table... one for each committee member and one for any witness who might be called to testify. An Assistant Sergeant-at-Arms is arranging the chairs around the table.

47 INT. THIRD FLOOR CORRIDOR - DAY

FEATURING Slattery as he exits his office and starts down the corridor toward the House chamber. He carries a thick bundle of papers and reports under one arm. Traffic along the corridor is fairly heavy. Slattery nods to a couple of people as he passes. Others glance at him coldly. This afternoon Slattery is not the most popular man in the legislature.

57.

48 INT. CORRIDOR - DAY

FEATURING Harry Sanborn and his wife as they make their way toward the main entrance to the House chamber. The corridor is crowded... there is much activity.

SANBORN
Honey, don't you think you'd be a lot more comfortable in the lounge? You can hear everything that goes on.

MARY
Thanks. I want to be in there. With you.

They start to move toward the main entrance and the Sergeant-at-Arms swings open the two huge doors and the Sanborns enter the chamber.

49 INT. THE HOUSE CHAMBER - DAY

CAMERA FOLLOWS Slattery as he enters from the side door and moves across the front of the chamber to the committee table where he sets his files down, then nods to Wills and Underwood who are already at the table.

SLATTERY
John... Stanley.

Wills and Underwood AD LIB their greetings.

50 THE HOUSE VISITORS' GALLERY

as Liz and Johnny enter. The gallery is crowded but they manage to find a couple of seats. CAMERA PANS over to Pat Russell who is already seated nearby.

51 THE FLOOR OF THE HOUSE

FEATURING Slattery as he looks across at Sanborn taking his seat.

METCAFF'S VOICE
The hour of 3:30 having arrived, we will proceed with Item number 1 on the Daily File, set as a special order of business for this time: The report of the special committee investigating certain charges against Representative Harry Sanborn. Representative Slattery, Chairman.

58.

52 ANOTHER ANGLE - FLOOR OF THE HOUSE

as Slattery turns, makes his way to his place at the committee table. He picks up a couple of sheets of paper containing notes for his opening remarks. Then he turns and faces the House.

SLATTERY
Mister Speaker... ladies and gentlemen of the House. You are well aware of the nature of the charges against Representative Sanborn which this committee was appointed to investigate.

NOTE: DURING SLATTERY'S SPEECH, CAMERA WILL CUT TO VARIOUS PRINCIPALS ON THE FLOOR AND IN THE GALLERY FOR REACTION SHOTS. THESE SHOULD INCLUDE: SANBORN, MARY SANBORN, LIZ AND JOHNNY, PAT RUSSELL, SPEAKER METCAFF, MAJORITY LEADER CARL BUTLER, FRANK RADCLIFF, AND SENATOR ELLIOTT.

SLATTERY
(continuing)
To begin with, I'd like to make one thing clear. The issue before us has nothing at all to do with the personalities involved. It has nothing at all to do with <u>why</u> Senator Elliott made this charge, or why he did it in such a spectacularly unusual fashion. The only question you may decide ,.. the only question you must decide is this: Did Representative Harry Sanborn deliberately, and with full knowledge of his act, violate the laws which govern the proceedings of this legislature.

Sanborn flings his desk microphone up and gets to his feet.

SANBORN
Mister Speaker?

METCAFF
Mister Sanborn... for what purpose do you rise?

(CONTINUED)

59.

52 CONTINUED

SANBORN
(bit sarcastic)
Mister Speaker... would you inquire if the prosecutor... excuse me... if Mister Slattery will yield for a question?

METCAFF
Mister Slattery... will you yield?

SLATTERY
Certainly.

SANBORN
Mister Slattery... I would like to know how the members of this body can decide the truth or falsity of these charges without regard to personalities, and especially without regard to motives? Are we not talking about human beings? About politicians? Are you asking this House to ignore the record and reputation of an ambitious young senator who talks more to the press and for the radio and the television cameras than he does to his own fellow legislators? Is it not true that many a politician has catapulted himself into national recognition by playing the part of the fearless investigator? Or are they better known as witch-hunters?

Metcaff POUNDS the gavel once.

METCAFF
Mister Sanborn... you will be given full opportunity to be heard. But it seems to me your question more than vaguely resembles a speech.

SANBORN
I apologize, sir, but Mister Slattery did yield for a question.

Metcaff glances at Slattery.

SLATTERY
Perhaps Mr. Sanborn can keep the length of his question within reason.

(CONTINUED)

60.

52 CONTINUED - (2):

SANBORN

Thank you, sir... as I hope you will keep your demands on this membership within reason. You ask the members of this House only to consider whether or not I sabotaged a piece of legislation. I contend when you judge a man you judge also his reputation. So how can you possibly ask this House to rule on this matter without considering the motives and past records of the people involved?

SLATTERY

I'll say it again, Mister Sanborn. Past records have nothing to do with the question at hand. I can't argue with your record, I can only envy it... and I'm sure that goes for the rest of the membership. If I remember correctly, over the years you've had a hand in writing and securing the passage of at least 60 pieces of major legislation. And you were the original author of half of them: a new child labor law, that was about 15 years ago... then came the Sanborn-Webber Labor Act... a new election code... the Sanborn-Fields Bill... then the Sanborn-Carter Housing Act... the Sanborn-Mc-Gloin Narcotics Law... And that's hardly a sampling of what you have accomplished in this House in the last 18 years. But I insist, Mr. Sanborn, we are not here to rate your qualities or your leadership... or your personal friendship. We're here to determine a single issue: Did you deliberately violate the laws of this legislature?

He walks to the table and picks up the committee report.

(CONTINUED)

52 CONTINUED - (3):

SLATTERY
(continuing)
Here is a report of the committee's findings. Here we indicate that there is a total lack of either formal or informal notes... no written evidence whatsoever... to show that the sub-committee report on Senate Bill 209 was ever voted on by the full membership of the Ways and Means Committee.

Sanborn is quickly on his feet once again. He speaks without benefit of a mike.

SANBORN
You know the answer to that as well as I do, Mister Slattery...

Metcaff GAVELS once again and Sanborn takes his seat.

SLATTERY
I know, Mister Sanborn. Plenty of mistakes are made in committee. Clerical and otherwise. But there are honest mistakes and there are the other kind.

Slattery pauses, tosses the report on the desk.

SLATTERY
(continuing)
This is a strange game we play up here, ladies and gentlemen. Politics. We maneuver, we deal, we compromise. That's the legislative process. But we have to stay within the rules... within the law. Because any time that any one of us violates those rules he's saying in effect, "I reject the legislative process." He's saying that the legislators who devote their lives and energies to the great struggle in these chambers are a bunch of fools play-acting in a tragic sham. Because there is no reason to debate, or compromise, or even vote if our legislative decisions are colored by fraud and deceit and then buried in a graveyard of lies.
(MORE)

(CONTINUED)

62.

52 CONTINUED - (4):

SLATTERY
(pauses)
You know a long time ago somebody said the whole art of legislation is the art of compromise. Well and good... it's a practical way of getting things done. But there are limitations. We can compromise on the contents of a bill anytime. But never... I repeat, never... can we compromise the rules we operate by. Morality. Political morality... that's what I'm talking about, ladies and gentlemen of the House. How long before we take a stand in that department? How long and how far do we back up before we stop and plant our feet and say, "To Hell with it! This is it! I'm not giving one more inch!" How long do we go on playing games with our collective conscience? And where... tell me where... do we draw the line between old-fashioned honesty and old-fashioned lying?

When Slattery finishes he is addressing Sanborn directly, or so it seems. Sanborn gets to his feet, raises his mike. The light on the arm of the mike flashes on.

METCAFF
Mister Sanborn?

SANBORN
Will the Minority Leader yield for a question?

SLATTERY
(clipped)
I yield.

SANBORN
Mister Slattery... do you mean to call me a liar?

SLATTERY
(quickly)
Those are your words - not mine.

(CONTINUED)

63.

52 CONTINUED - (5):

Metcaff GAVELS once but Sanborn is insistent, angry, his voice raised.

SANBORN
Do you mean to call me a liar?

SLATTERY
Yes sir, I do.

Metcaff GAVELS again.

METCAFF
That is an improper question.

SANBORN
Then prove it, Mister Slattery!
Prove it!

Metcaff is quietly irked, GAVELS once more.

METCAFF
You are out of order, Mister
Sanborn.

Sanborn sits down, trembling with rage. Slattery looks at him, then turns and moves back to the committee table.

SLATTERY
Mister Speaker, we have a single
witness to call... the Director
of State Parks, Mister Alan
Morrow.

Alan Morrow is ushered in from one of the side entrances by a Sergeant-at-Arms. He moves up to the Committee table's witness chair where the Clerk administers the oath and Morrow is then seated.

SLATTERY
(continuing)
Mister Morrow, did Representative
Sanborn ever speak to you about
Senate Bill 209... the bill
authored by Senator Elliott?

MORROW
Yes, he did.

(CONTINUED)

64.

52 CONTINUED - (6):

SLATTERY
What did he say?

MORROW
He told me to use my influence
to have the Warm Valley area
eliminated from the plans for
the proposed state park.

SLATTERY
Did he state what the consequences would be if you did
not go along with his request?

MORROW
He threatened to kill the bill
in committee if Warm Valley was
not excluded from the plans.

SLATTERY
Why did he want to retain Warm
Valley? Was it because he
didn't want the land dropped
from his county's tax rolls?

MORROW
No, sir. That wasn't the real
reason.

SLATTERY
Then what is?

MORROW
Because the farmers and the
irrigation district down there
want to build a dam in Warm Valley.

SLATTERY
A dam?

MORROW
Yes. With the amount of water
they'd get from a project like
that they could at least double
the farm income for their county.

SLATTERY
But the farmers down there are
getting more than their fair
share of water right now, isn't
that correct? Their farm income
is one of the highest in the state.

(CONTINUED)

52 CONTINUED - (7):

MORROW
I guess they want to have <u>the</u> highest.

SLATTERY
Mr. Morrow, would you tell us how you happened to obtain this information?

MORROW
Well, in order to make sure they had the proper sub-surface soil on which to erect a dam the county surveyors had to make a series of core-drillings in the Warm Valley area. At the time, it so happened that three men from my department were looking over the area in connection with the proposed state park. They saw the county survey team at work and it became fairly obvious what the county had in mind.

Sanborn is on his feet again.

SANBORN
Mister Speaker..?

METCAFF
You will have the opportunity to cross-examine the witness if you so desire, Mister Sanborn.
(turns)
Continue, Mister Slattery.

SLATTERY
Mister Morrow, did Representative Sanborn, on at least one occasion, talk to you by telephone about Senate Bill 209?

MORROW
Yes.

SLATTERY
Do you have a record of that phone call?

MORROW
(after a pause)
We have a recording.

(CONTINUED)

66.

52 CONTINUED - (8):

Slattery takes a small reel of tape from his pocket, shows it to Morrow.

SLATTERY

I ask you to testify that this is the original tape recording of that phone call.

MORROW

Yes.

Slattery crosses to a tape-recorder which has been set up on the table and so wired that it feeds into the House loud-speaker system. He threads the tape onto the machine and pushes the "start" button. NOTE: DURING THE COURSE OF THE ENSUING RECORDING, CAMERA WILL CUT TO OUR PRINCIPALS FOR REACTION SHOTS. The first thing we HEAR on the recording is the SOUND of a BUZZER followed by the SOUND of a phone receiver being lifted.

SECRETARY'S VOICE

(recorded; heard over P.A.)

Representative Sanborn calling you, Mister Morrow.

MORROW'S VOICE

(brief pause)

All right. Put him on.

There is a CLICK. When Sanborn's voice is heard, there is no mistaking it. He comes over loud and clear.

MORROW

Hello?

SANBORN'S VOICE

(recorded; heard over P.A.)

Morrow, this is Harry Sanborn. I called to make sure you changed your mind about Elliott's park bill...

MORROW

(hesitant)

Well, as a matter of fact, Mister Sanborn, I haven't changed my mind. I think...

(CONTINUED)

52 CONTINUED - (9):

SANBORN
(breaking in)
Morrow, I'm telling you for the last time. You make sure that the Warm Valley area is cut out of the plans or you'll end up with no park at all. Is that clear?

MORROW
But the Senate passed the bill, Mister Sanborn. Unanimously. And I understand that...

SANBORN
(breaking in)
You understand me. That bill has to come through Ways and Means committee. I'm chairman of that committee, Morrow. I run it. So cut Warm Valley out of the plans or the bill is dead.

We hear the SOUND of the phone being hung up. Slattery reaches over and turns off the tape machine. There is a complete and utter silence throughout the huge chamber. Sanborn is ashen, mute. There is no sense of triumph or victory, either in word or action as Slattery makes the first move. He picks up a copy of the committee report from the table, then turns and walks directly in front of the rostrum and faces the Speaker.

SLATTERY
This is the report of your committee, Mister Speaker. The recommendation is unanimous and it reads as follows: 'That the charges lodged by Senator Elliott against Representative Harry Sanborn, a member of this House, are well taken... that they are founded in truth and in fact, and that appropriate action be taken against the offending member. The committee also recommends that Representative Sanborn be removed from his position as Chairman of the Ways and Means Committee of this House'.

He hands the report to the Clerk who in turn passes it up to the Speaker's rostrum.

(CONTINUED)

68.

52 CONTINUED - (10):

SLATTERY
(continuing;
firmly, clearly)
Mister Speaker, I move that the
report of this committee be
adopted by the House.

After a pause, the Speaker looks out over the membership.

METCAFF
Is there a second to the motion?

There is a long pause and then somewhere in the middle of the House we HEAR but do not see Carl Butler.

BUTLER'S VOICE
Second.

METCAFF
The motion has been made and
seconded that we adopt the
committee report.
(pause)
Is there any further discussion?

There is only silence. Finally, as if to say 'this is the least I can do', the Speaker turns and looks down at Sanborn.

METCAFF
(continuing)
Mister Sanborn?

Like a sleep-walker, Harry gets to his feet, raises his microphone. His voice is choked, he has aged 10 years in the period of an hour.

SANBORN
Only this, Mister Speaker. I
was elected by the people of
the 21st District to represent
them in this House. My first
duty is to them. I can see it
no other way. They are my people
and I was sent here to speak for
them. Over the years I have spoken
for them. I have represented them.
I have fought for them. With all
my might, with all my energies.
Ladies and gentlemen of the House
... if this be a crime... then I
stand guilty.

(CONTINUED)

69.

52 CONTINUED - (11):

Slowly, he pushes his mike down but he remains standing. He doesn't seem to know whether to sit down, remain standing or what. He stares dumbly at his desk, looks up, turns and starts down the aisle toward the rear of the chamber.

53 MED. CLOSE TWO SHOT - SANBORN AND MARY

as he moves up to where she is seated. Her eyes brim with tears. Harry's voice is a hoarse whisper.

SANBORN
Mary... Time to go.

She gets to her feet, eyes him closely. At this moment she loves him more than she ever has or ever will again. She takes his arm.

MARY
Yes. It's time.

They start to move out of the chamber and the two Sergeants-at-Arms, a bit nervous and bewildered, hold open the two huge doors as they exit.

54 ANOTHER ANGLE - THE HOUSE CHAMBER

CAMERA SHOOTING past Slattery, who is now at his regular desk, and featuring the rostrum.

METCAFF
There being no further discussion,
the Clerk will prepare the roll
for a vote on Mister Slattery's
motion. 41 votes are needed.

We HEAR them sound the roll being prepared, the GONG sounds, but after a long pause no voting lights appear on the board... neither in the "aye" or "no" vote columns. The Speaker is unsure of himself.

METCAFF
(continuing)
The roll is prepared, gentlemen.
We are ready to vote.

CAMERA PANS AROUND the floor and we pick up some reactions of some principals. CAMERA finally rests on Slattery. It's sheer torture but he reaches forward, flips the switch covering his voting buttons to an "open" position. He pauses briefly again, then deliberately and firmly he pushes down on the "aye" button. Ponderously at first and then gaining momentum... the voting starts. Finally, there are 79 green lights (aye) showing on the big board.

70.

55 THE HOUSE GALLERY

FEATURING Johnny and Liz, who is teary-eyed. We see Pat Russell exit. Tears are streaming down her face.

56 FLOOR OF THE HOUSE

FEATURING Slattery as the roll is closed and the votes tallied.

METCAFF
Ayes... 79. No's... none.
The motion is adopted.

Cautiously, Senator Elliott crosses the chamber and moves up to Slattery's desk. He's about as ingratiating as a novice funeral director.

ELLIOTT
Slattery?

Slattery looks up.

ELLIOTT
(continuing)
I know you don't feel much like talking, but I just had to come over and compliment you. It was a rough job. It must have taken a lot of courage.

Slattery looks at him with loathing and disdain.

SLATTERY
How would you know? Senator.

He gets to his feet, brushes by Elliott, almost knocking him over, and heads for the side door.

57 INT. CORRIDOR

This is the corridor adjoining the side entrance to the House. As Slattery emerges he hears Pat call his name. She is still a bit teary.

PAT
Slattery...

Slattery turns.

(CONTINUED)

71.

57 CONTINUED

PAT
(continuing)
You're a man, Slattery. That's the best thing I can possibly say about you. You're a man.

She turns and moves off. Slattery looks after her for a moment, then turns and heads in the opposite direction.

58 INT. FIRST FLOOR

as Slattery makes his way toward the doors coming TOWARD CAMERA. To one side the elevator doors open, Johnny emerges alone and crosses to Slattery. They continue moving toward the doors.

SLATTERY
It's about time you went home.

JOHNNY
(grins)
Been a long day.

Slattery pauses at the door to light a cigarette. Johnny does likewise.

SLATTERY
You've seen quite a show in the few weeks you've been up here, John. Democracy in action... all that bit. What do you think of it?

JOHNNY
You mean today?

SLATTERY
(grunts)
That's a fair sample. How'd it strike you?

JOHNNY
(slight shrug)
Offhand it seems to be a tough way to run a country.

SLATTERY
(slight smile)
That's right. But then who ever promised us it was going to be easy?

(CONTINUED)

72.

58 CONTINUED

Slattery turns and starts off.

DISSOLVE:

59 EXT. MAIN ENTRANCE OF CAPITOL - NIGHT

CAMERA HOLDING on Slattery as he makes his way wearily down the steps. As he reaches the path which leads down to the street, the lights along the path are suddenly turned on. Slattery turns and looks back. The lights on the capitol dome are turned on. Slattery reacts somewhat enigmatically. Then he turns and moves off into the dark.

FADE OUT

THE END